S0-BMZ-419

BLACKFEET

INDIAN STORIES

BY

GEORGE BIRD GRINNELL

AUTHOR OF

"BLACKFEET LODGE TALES," "TRAILS OF THE PATHFINDERS," ETC.

WILDER BRANCH LIBRARY
7140 E. SEVEN MILE RD.
DETROIT, MI 48234 — 876-0136

NEW YORK

CHARLES SCRIBNER'S SONS

1926

398.20899
G885b

WILDER BRANCH LIBRARY
7140 E. SEVEN MILE RD.
DETROIT, MI 48234 — 876-0136

COPYRIGHT, 1913, BY
CHARLES SCRIBNER'S SONS

Printed in the United States of America

WI   MAY   '95

TO THE READER

Those who wish to know something about how the people lived who told these stories will find their ways of life described in the last chapter of this book

The Blackfeet were hunters, travelling from place to place on foot. They used implements of stone, wood, or bone, wore clothing made of skins, and lived in tents covered by hides. Dogs, their only tame animals, were used as beasts of burden to carry small packs and drag light loads.

The stories here told come down to us from very ancient times. Grandfathers have told them to their grandchildren, and these again to their grandchildren, and so from mouth to mouth, through many generations, they have reached our time.

CONTENTS

CONTENTS

BLACKFEET INDIAN STORIES

Blackfeet Indian Stories

TWO FAST RUNNERS

ONCE, a long time ago, the antelope and the deer happened to meet on the prairie. They spoke together, giving each other the news, each telling what he had seen and done. After they had talked for a time the antelope told the deer how fast he could run, and the deer said that he could run fast too, and before long each began to say that he could run faster than the other. So they agreed that they would have a race to decide which could run the faster, and on this race they bet their galls. When they started, the antelope ran ahead of the deer from the very start and won the race and so took the deer's gall.

But the deer began to grumble and said, "Well, it is true that out here on the prairie

1

you have beaten me, but this is not where I live. I only come out here once in a while to feed or to cross the prairie when I am going somewhere. It would be fairer if we had a race in the timber. That is my home, and there I can run faster than you. I am sure of it."

The antelope felt so glad and proud that he had beaten the deer in the race that he was sure that wherever they might run he could beat him, so he said, "All right, I will run you a race in the timber. I have beaten you out here on the flat and I can beat you there." On this race they bet their dew-claws.

They started and ran this race through the thick timber, among the bushes, and over fallen logs, and this time the antelope ran slowly, for he was afraid of hitting himself against the trees or of falling over the logs. You see, he was not used to this kind of travelling. So the deer easily beat him and took his dew-claws.

Since that time the deer has had no gall and the antelope no dew-claws.

THE WOLF MAN

A LONG time ago there was a man who had two wives. They were not good women; they did not look after their home nor try to keep things comfortable there. If the man brought in plenty of buffalo cow skins they did not tan them well, and often when he came home at night, hungry and tired after his hunting, he had no food, for these women would be away from the lodge, visiting their relations and having a good time.

The man thought that if he moved away from the big camp and lived alone where there were no other people perhaps he might teach these women to become good; so he moved his lodge far off on the prairie and camped at the foot of a high butte.

Every evening about sundown the man used to climb up to the top of this butte and sit there and look all over the country to see where

3

the buffalo were feeding and whether any enemies were moving about. On top of the hill there was a buffalo skull, on which he used to sit.

One day one of the women said to the other, "It is very lonely here; we have no one to talk with or to visit."

"Let us kill our husband," said the other; "then we can go back to our relations and have a good time."

Early next morning the man set out to hunt, and as soon as he was out of sight his wives went up on top of the butte where he used to sit. There they dug a deep hole and covered it over with light sticks and grass and earth, so that it looked like the other soil near by, and placed the buffalo skull on the sticks which covered the hole.

In the afternoon, as they watched for their returning husband, they saw him come over the hill loaded down with meat that he had killed. When he threw down his load outside the lodge, they hurried to cook something for him. After he had eaten he went up on the butte and sat down on the skull. The slender sticks broke and he fell into the hole. His wives were watching him, and when they saw him disappear, they took down the lodge and packed their dogs and set out to go to the main camp. As they drew near it, so that people could hear them, they began to cry and mourn.

Soon some people came to meet them and said, "What is this? Why are you mourning? Where is your husband?"

"Ah," they replied, "he is dead. Five days ago he went out to hunt and he did not come back. What shall we do? We have lost him who cared for us"; and they cried and mourned again.

Now, when the man fell into the pit he was hurt, for the hole was deep. After a time he tried to climb out, but he was so badly bruised that he could not do so. He sat there and waited, thinking that here he must surely die of hunger.

But travelling over the prairie was a wolf that climbed up on the butte and came to the hole and, looking in, saw the man and pitied him.

"Ah-h-w-o-o-o! Ah-h-w-o-o-o-o!" he howled, and when the other wolves heard him they all came running to see what was the matter. Following the big wolves came also many coyotes, badgers, and kit-foxes. They did not know what had happened, but they thought perhaps there was food here.

To the others the wolf said, "Here in this hole is what I have found. Here is a man who has fallen in. Let us dig him out and we will have him for our brother."

All the wolves thought that this talk was good, and they began to dig, and before very long they had dug a hole down almost to the bottom of the pit.

Then the wolf who had found the man said, "Hold on; wait a little; I want to say a few words." All the animals stopped digging and began to listen, and the wolf said, "We will all have this man for our brother; but I found him, and so I think he ought to live with us big wolves." All the others thought that this was good, and the wolf that had found the man went into the hole that had been dug, and tearing down the rest of the earth, dragged out the poor man, who was now almost dead, for he had neither eaten nor drunk anything since he fell in the hole. They gave the man a kidney to eat, and when he was able to walk the big wolves took him to their home. Here there was a very old blind wolf who had great power and could do wonderful things. He cured the man and made his head and his hands look like those of a wolf. The rest of his body was not changed.

In those days the people used to make holes in the walls of the fence about the enclosure into which they led the buffalo. They set snares over these holes, and when wolves and other animals crept through them so as to get into the pen and feed on the meat they were caught by the neck and killed, and the people used their skins for clothing.

One night all the wolves went down to the pen to get meat, and when they had come close to it, the man-wolf said to his brothers, "Stop here for a little while and I will go down and fix the places so that you will not be caught." He went down to the pen and sprung all the snares, and then went back and called the wolves and the others—the coyotes, badgers, and kit-foxes—and they all went into the pen and feasted and took meat to carry home to their families. In the morning the people found the meat gone and all their snares sprung, and they were surprised and wondered how this could have happened. For many nights the nooses were pulled tight and the meat taken; but once when the wolves went there to eat they found only the meat of a lean and sickly bull. Then the man-wolf was angry, and he cried out like a wolf, "Bad-food-you-give-us-o-o-o! Bad-food-you-give-us-o-o-o-o!"

When the people heard this they said to one another, "Ah, it is a man-wolf who has done all this. We must catch him." So they took down to the piskun[1] pemmican and nice back fat and placed it there, and many of them hid

[1] A pen or enclosure, usually—among the Blackfeet—at the foot of a cliff, over which the buffalo were induced to jump. Pronounced pi'skŭn.

close by. After dark the wolves came, as was their custom, and when the man-wolf saw the good food, he ran to it and began to eat. Then the people rushed upon him from every side and caught him with ropes, and tied him and took him to a lodge, and when they had brought him inside to the light of the fire, at once they knew who it was. They said, "Why, this is the man who was lost."

"No," said the man, "I was not lost. My wives tried to kill me. They dug a deep hole and I fell into it, and I was hurt so badly I could not get out; but the wolves took pity on me and helped me or I would have died there."

When the people heard this they were angry, and they told the man to do something to punish these women.

"You say well," he replied; "I give those women to the punishing society. They know what to do."

After that night the two women were never seen again.

KŬT-O-YĬS', THE BLOOD BOY

AS the children whose ancestors came from
Europe have stories about the heroes who
killed wicked and cruel monsters—like Jack the
Giant Killer, for example—so the Indian children hear stories about persons who had magic
power and who went about the world destroying those who treated cruelly or killed the Indians of the camps. Such a hero was Kŭt-o-
yĭs', and this is how he came to be alive and
to travel about from place to place, helping the
people and destroying their enemies.

It was long, long ago, down where Two Medicine and Badger Rivers come together, that an
old man lived with his wife and three daughters.
One day there came to his camp a young man,
good-looking, a good hunter, and brave. He
stayed in the camp for some time, and whenever he went hunting he killed game and
brought in great loads of meat.

10

All this time the old man was watching him, for he said in his heart, "This seems a good young man and a good hunter. Perhaps I will give him my daughters for wives, and then he will stay here and help me always."

After a time the old man decided to do this, and he gave the young man his daughters; and because these three were his only children he gave his son-in-law his dogs and all his property, and for himself and his wife he kept only a little lodge. The young man's wives tanned plenty of cow skins and made a big fine lodge, and in this the son-in-law lived with his wives.

For some time after this the son-in-law was very good and kind to the old people. When he killed any animal he gave them part of the meat, and gave them skins which his mother-in-law tanned for robes or for clothing.

As time went on the son-in-law began to grow stingy, and pretty soon he gave nothing to his father-in-law's lodge, but kept everything for his own.

Now, the son-in-law was a person of much mysterious power, and he kept the buffalo hidden under a big log-jam in the river. Whenever he needed food and wished to kill anything, he would take his father-in-law with him to help. He would send the old man out to stamp on the log-jam and frighten the buffalo, and when they ran out from under it the young man would shoot one or two with his arrows, never killing more than he needed. But often he gave the old people nothing at all to eat. They were hungry all the time, and at length they began to grow thin and weak.

One morning early the young man asked his father-in-law to come and hunt with him. They went to the log-jam and the old man drove out the buffalo and his son-in-law killed a fat buffalo cow. Then he said to his father-in-law, "Hurry back now to the camp and tell your daughters to come and carry home the meat, and then you can have something to eat." The old man set out for the camp, thinking, as he walked along, "Now, at last, my son-in-law has taken pity on me; he will give me some of this meat."

When he returned with his daughters they

12

skinned the cow and cut it up and, carrying it, went home. The young man had his wives leave the meat at his own lodge and told his father-in-law to go home. He did not give him even a little piece of the meat. The two older daughters gave their parents nothing to eat, but sometimes the youngest one had pity on them and took a piece of meat and, when she could, threw it into the lodge to the old people. The son-in-law had told his wives not to give the old people anything to eat. Except for the good heart of the youngest daughter they would have died of hunger.

Another day the son-in-law rose early in the morning and went over to the old man's lodge and kicked against the poles, calling to him, "Get up now and help me; I want you to go and stamp on the log-jam to drive out the buffalo." When the old man moved his feet on the jam and a buffalo ran out, the son-in-law was not ready for it, and it passed by him before he shot the arrow; so he only wounded it. It ran away, but at last it fell down and died.

13

The old man followed close after it, and as he ran along he came to a place where a great clot of blood had fallen from the buffalo's wound. When he came to where this clot of blood was lying on the ground, he stumbled and fell and spilled his arrows out of his quiver, and while he was picking them up he picked up also the clot of blood and hid it in his quiver.

"What are you picking up?" called the son-in-law.

"Nothing," replied the old man. "I fell down and spilled my arrows, and I am putting them back."

"Ah, old man," said the son-in-law, "you are lazy and useless. You no longer help me. Go back now to the camp and tell your daughters to come down here and help carry in this meat."

The old man went to the camp and told his daughters of the meat that their husband had killed, and they went down to the killing ground. Then he went to his own lodge and said to his wife, "Hurry, now, put the stone kettle on the fire. I have brought home something from the killing."

"Ah," said the old woman, "has our son-in-law been generous and given us something nice to eat?"

"No," replied the old man, "but hurry and put the kettle on the fire."

After a time the water began to boil and the old man turned his quiver upside down over the pot, and immediately there came from it a sound of a child crying, as if it were being hurt. The old people both looked in the kettle and there they saw a little boy, and they quickly took him out of the water. They were surprised and did not know where the child had come from. The old woman wrapped the child up and wound a line about its wrappings to keep them in place, making a lashing for the child. Then they talked about it, wondering what should be done with it. They thought that if their son-in-law knew it was a boy he would kill it; so they determined to tell their daughters that the baby was a girl, for then their son-in-law would think that he was going to have another wife. So he would be glad. They called the child Kŭt-o-yĭs'—Clot of Blood.

The son-in-law and his wives came home, bringing the meat, and after a little time they heard the child in the next lodge crying. The son-in-law said to his youngest wife, "Go over to your mother's and see whether that baby is a boy or a girl. If it is a boy, tell your parents to kill it."

Soon the young woman came back and said to her husband, "It is a girl baby. You are to have another wife."

The son-in-law did not know whether to believe this, and sent his oldest wife to ask the same question. When she came back and told him the same thing he believed that it was really a girl. Then he was glad, for he said to himself, "Now, when this child has grown up, I shall have another wife." He said to his youngest wife, "Take some back fat and pemmican over to your mother; she must be well fed now that she has to nurse this child."

On the fourth day after he had been born the child spoke and said to his mother, "Hold me in turn to each one of these lodge poles, and when I come to the last one I shall fall out of

my lashings and be grown up." The old woman
did as he had said, and as she held him to one
pole after another he could be seen to grow;
and finally when he was held to the last pole he
was a man.

After Kŭt-o-yĭs' had looked about the lodge
he put his eye to a hole in the lodge-covering and
looked out. Then he turned around and said
to the old people, "How is it that in this lodge
there is nothing to eat? Over by the other
lodge I see plenty of food hanging up."

"Hush," said the old woman, raising her
hand, "you will be heard. Our son-in-law lives
over there. He does not give us anything at
all to eat."

"Well," said the young man, "where is your
piskun—where do you kill buffalo?"

"It is down by the river," the old woman answered. "We pound on it and the buffalo run
out."

For some time they talked together and the
old man told Kŭt-o-yĭs' how his son-in-law had
abused him. He said to the young man, "He
has taken from me my bow and my arrows and

has taken even my dogs; and now for many days we have had nothing to eat, except sometimes a small piece of meat that our daughter throws to us."

"Father," said Kŭt-o-yĭs′, "have you no arrows?"

"No, my son," replied the old man, "but I still have four stone arrow points."

"Go out then," said Kŭt-o-yĭs′, "and get some wood. We will make a bow and some arrows, and in the morning we will go down to where the buffalo are and kill something to eat."

Early in the morning Kŭt-o-yĭs′ pushed the old man and said, "Come, get up now, and we will go down and kill, when the buffalo come out." It was still very early in the morning.

When they reached the river the old man said, "This is the place to stand and shoot. I will go down and drive them out."

He went down and stamped on the log-jam, and presently a fat cow ran out and Kŭt-o-yĭs′ killed it.

Now, after these two had gone to the river

the son-in-law arose and went over to the old
man's lodge, and knocked on the poles and called
to the old man to get up and help him kill. The
old woman called out to the son-in-law, saying,
"Your father-in-law has already gone down to
the piskun." This made the son-in-law angry,
and he began to talk badly to the old woman
and to threaten to harm her.

Presently he went on down to the log-jam,
and as he got near the place he saw the old man
at work there, bending over, skinning a buffalo;
for Kŭt-o-yĭs', when he had seen the son-in-law
coming, had lain down on the ground and hidden himself behind the carcass.

When the son-in-law had come pretty close
to where the buffalo lay he said to his father-in-
law, "Old man, stand up and look all about
you. Look carefully and well, for it will be the
last time that you will ever see anything"; and
while the son-in-law said this he took an arrow
from his quiver.

Kŭt-o-yĭs' spoke to the old man from his hid-
ing-place and said, "Tell your son-in-law that
he must take his last look, for that you are going

to kill him now." The old man said this as he had been told.

"Ah," said the son-in-law, "you talk back to me. That makes me still angrier at you." He put an arrow on the string and shot at the old man, but did not hit him. Kŭt-o-yĭs' said to the old man, "Pick up that arrow and shoot it back at him"; and the old man did so. Now, they shot at each other four times, and then the old man said to Kŭt-o-yĭs', "I am afraid now; get up and help me. If you do not, I think he will kill me." Then Kŭt-o-yĭs' rose to his feet and said to the son-in-law, "Here, what are you doing? I think you have been treating this old man badly for a long time. Why do you do it?"

"Oh no," said the son-in-law, and he smiled at Kŭt-o-yĭs' in a friendly way, for he was afraid of him. "Oh no; no one thinks more of this old man than I do. I have always been very good to him."

"No," said Kŭt-o-yĭs'. "You are saying what is not true, and I am going to kill you now."

Kŭt-o-yĭs' shot the son-in-law four times and

he fell down and died. Then the young man told his father to go and bring down to him the daughters who had acted badly toward him. The old man did so and Kŭt-o-yĭs´ punished them. Then he went up to the lodges and said to the youngest woman, "Did you love your husband?" "Yes," said the girl, "I loved him." So Kŭt-o-yĭs´ punished her too, but not so badly as he had the other daughters, because she had been kind to her parents.

To the old people he said, "Go over now to that lodge and live there. There is plenty of food, and when that is gone I will kill more. As for me, I shall make a journey. Tell me where there are any people. In what direction shall I go to find a camp?"

"Well," said the old man, "up here on Two Medicine Lodge Creek there are some people —up where the piskun is, you know."

Kŭt-o-yĭs´ followed up the stream to where the piskun was and there found many lodges of people. In the centre of the camp was a big lodge, and painted on it the figure of a bear He did not go to this lodge, but went into a small lodge where two old women lived. When he had sat down they put food before him— lean dried meat and some belly fat.

"How is this, grandmothers?" he said. "Here is a camp with plenty of fat meat and back fat hanging up to dry; why do you not give me some of that?"

"Hush; be careful," said the old women. "In that big lodge over there lives a big bear and his wives and children. He takes all the best food and leaves us nothing. He is the chief of this place."

Early in the morning Kŭt-o-yĭs' said to the old women, "Harness up your dogs to the tra- vois now and go over to the piskun, and I will kill some fat meat for you."

When they got there, he killed a fat cow and helped the old women to cut it up, and they took it to the lodge. One of those old women said, "Ah me, the bears will be sure to come."

"Why do you say that?" he asked.

They said to him, "We shall be sorry to lose this back fat."

"Do not fear," he said. "No one shall take

22

this back fat from you. Now, take all those best pieces and hang them up, so that those who live in the bear lodge may see them."

They did so. Pretty soon the old bear chief said to one of his children, "By this time I think the people have finished killing. Go out now and look about; see where the nicest pieces are, and bring in some nice back fat."

One of the young bears went out of the lodge and stood up and looked about, and when it saw this meat hanging by the old women's lodge close by, it went over toward it.

"Ah," said the old women, "there are those bears."

"Do not be afraid," said Kŭt-o-yĭs'.

The young bear went over to where the meat was hanging and stood up and began to pull it down. Kŭt-o-yĭs' went out of the lodge and said, "Wait; wait! What are you doing, taking the old women's meat?"

The young bear answered, "My father told me that I should go out and get this meat and bring it home to him."

Kŭt-o-yĭs′ hit the young bear over the head with a stick and it ran home crying.

When it had reached the lodge it told what had happened and the father bear said, "I will go over there myself; perhaps this person will hit me over the head."

When the old women saw the father and mother bear and all their relations coming they were afraid, but Kŭt-o-yĭs′ jumped out of the lodge and killed the bears one after another; all except one little she-bear, a very small one, which got away.

"Well," said Kŭt-o-yĭs′, "you may go and breed more bears."

He told the old women to move over to the bear-painted lodge and after this to live in it. It was theirs.

To the old women Kŭt-o-yĭs′ then said, "Now, grandmothers, where are there any more people? I want to travel about and see them."

The old women said, "At the Point of Rocks —on Sun River—there is a camp. There is a piskun there."

So Kŭt-o-yĭs′ set off for that place, and when

he came to the camp he went into an old woman's lodge.

The old woman gave him something to eat —a dish of bad food.

"Why is this, grandmother?" asked Kŭt-o-yĭs'. "Have you no food better than this to give to a visitor? Down there I see a piskun; you must kill plenty of buffalo and must have good food."

"Speak lower," said the old woman, "or you may be heard. We have no good food because there is a great snake here who is the chief of the camp. He takes all the best pieces. He lives over there in that snake-painted lodge."

The next morning when the buffalo were led in, Kŭt-o-yĭs' killed one, and they took the back fat and carried it to their lodge. Then Kŭt-o-yĭs' said, "I think I will visit that snake person." He went over and went into the lodge, and there he saw many women that the snake person had taken to be his wives. The women were cooking some service berries. Kŭt-o-yĭs' picked up the dish and ate the berries and threw the dish away. Then he went up to the big snake, who was lying there asleep, and pricked him with his knife, saying, "Here, get up; I have come to visit you. Let us smoke together."

Then the snake was angry and he raised up his head and began to rattle, and Kŭt-o-yĭs' cut off his head and cut him in pieces. He cut off the heads of all the snake's wives and children; all except one little female snake which got away by crawling into a crack in the rocks.

"Oh, well," said Kŭt-o-yĭs', "you can go and breed snakes so there will be more. The people will not be afraid of little snakes."

Kŭt-o-yĭs' said to the old woman, "Now, grandmother, go into this snake lodge and take it for your own and everything that is in it."

Then he said to them, "Where are there some more people?" They told him there were some camps down the river and some up in the mountains, but they said, "Do not go up there. It is bad because there lives Āi-sīn'-o-kō-kī— Wind Sucker. He will kill you."

Kŭt-o-yĭs' was glad to know that there was such a person, and he went to the mountains.

When he reached the place where Wind Sucker

lived, he looked into his mouth and saw there many dead people. Some were skeletons and some had only just died. He went in, and there he saw a fearful sight. The ground was white as snow with the bones of those who had died. There were bodies with flesh on them; some who had died not long before and some who were still living.

As he looked about, he saw hanging down above him a great thing that seemed to move— to grow a little larger and then to grow a little smaller.

Kŭt-o-yĭs' spoke to one of the people who was alive and asked, "What is that hanging down above us?"

The person answered him, "That is Wind Sucker's heart."

Then Kŭt-o-yĭs' spoke to all the living and said to them, "You who still draw a little breath try to move your heads in time to the song that I shall sing; and you who are still able to move stand up on your feet and dance. Take courage now; we are going to dance to the ghosts."

Then Kŭt-o-yĭs' tied his knife, point upward

to the top of his head and began to dance, singing the ghost song, and all the others danced with him; and as he danced up and down he kept springing higher and higher into the air, and the point of his knife cut Wind Sucker's heart and killed him.

Then Kŭt-o-yĭs', with his knife, cut a hole between Wind Sucker's ribs, and he and all those who were able to move crawled out through the hole. He said to those who could still walk that they should go and tell their people to come here, to get the ones still alive but unable to travel.

To some of these people that he had freed he said, "Where are there any other people? I want to visit all the people."

"There is a camp to the westward, up the river," they replied; "but you must not take the left-hand trail going up because on that trail lives a woman who invites men to wrestle with her and then kills them. Avoid her."

Now, really, this was what Kŭt-o-yĭs' was looking for. This was what he was doing in the world, trying to kill off all the bad things.

He asked these people just where this woman lived and how it was best for him to go so that he should not meet her. He did this because he did not wish the people to know that he was going where she was.

He started, and after he had travelled some time he saw a woman standing not far from the trail. She called to him, saying, "Come here, young man, come here; I want to wrestle with you."

"No," he replied, "I am in a hurry; I cannot stop."

The woman called again, "No, no; do not go on; come now and wrestle once with me."

After she had called him the fourth time, Kŭt-o-yĭs' went to her.

Now on the ground where this woman wrestled with people she had placed many sharp, broken flint-stones, partly hiding them by the grass. The two seized each other and began to wrestle over these sharp stones, but Kŭt-o-yĭs' looked at the ground and did not step on them. He watched his chance and gave the woman a quick wrench, and threw her down on

29

a, large sharp flint which cut her in two; and the parts of her body fell asunder.

Kŭt-o-yĭs' then went on, and after a time came to where a woman had made a place for sliding downhill. At the far end of it she had fixed a rope which, when she raised it, would trip people up, and when they were tripped they fell over a high cliff into a deep water, where a great fish ate them.

When this woman saw Kŭt-o-yĭs' coming she cried out to him, "Come over here, young man, and slide with me."

"No," he replied, "I am in a hurry; I cannot wait." She kept calling to him, and when she had called him the fourth time he went over where he was to slide with her.

"This sliding," said the woman, "is very good fun."

"Ah, yes," said Kŭt-o-yĭs', "I will look at it."

As he went near the place he looked carefully and saw the hidden rope. He began to slide, and holding his knife in his hand, when he reached the rope he cut it just as the woman raised it and pulled on it, and the woman fell over backward into the water and was eaten up by the big fish.

From here he went on again, and after a time he came to a big camp. A man-eater was the chief of this place.

Before Kŭt-o-yĭs' went to the chief's lodge he looked about and saw a little girl and called her to him and said, "Child, I am going into that lodge, to let that man-eater kill and eat me. Therefore, be on the watch, and if you can get hold of one of my bones take it out and call all the dogs to you, and when they have come to you throw down the bone and say, 'Kŭt-o-yis', the dogs are eating your bones.'"

Then Kŭt-o-yĭs' entered the lodge, and when the man-eater saw him he called out, "Oki, oki!" (welcome, welcome!) and seemed glad to see him, for he was a fat young man. The man-eater took a knife and walked up to Kŭt-o-yĭs' and cut his throat and put him into a great stone pot to cook. When the meat was cooked he pulled the kettle from the fire and ate the body, limb by limb, until it was all eaten.

After that the little girl who was watching

came into the lodge and said, "Pity me, man-eater, my mother is hungry and asks you for those bones." The old man gathered them together and handed them to her, and she took them out of the lodge. When she had gone a little way, she called all the dogs to her and threw down the bones to the dogs, crying out, "Look out, Kŭt-o-yĭs', the dogs are eating you," and when she said that, Kŭt-o-yĭs' arose from the pile of bones.

Again he went into the lodge, and when the man-eater saw him he cried out, "How, how, how! the fat young man has survived!" and he seemed surprised. Again he took his knife and cut the throat of Kŭt-o-yĭs' and threw him into the kettle. Again when the meat was cooked he ate it, and when the little girl asked for the bones again he gave them to her. She took them out and threw them to the dogs, crying, "Kŭt-o-yĭs', the dogs are eating you," and again Kŭt-o-yĭs' arose from the bones.

When the man-eater had cooked him four times Kŭt-o-yĭs' again went into the lodge, and seizing the man-eater, he threw him into the boiling kettle, and his wives and all his children, and boiled them to death.

The man-eater was the seventh and last of the bad things to be destroyed by Kŭt-o-yĭs'.

THE DOG AND THE ROOT DIGGER

THIS happened long ago.

In those days the people were hungry. No buffalo could be found, no antelope were seen on the prairie. Grass grew in the trails where the elk and the deer used to travel. There was not even a rabbit in the brush. Then the people prayed, "Oh, Napi, help us now or we must die. The buffalo and the deer are gone. It is useless to kindle the morning fires; our arrows are useless to us; our knives remain in their sheaths."

Then Napi set out to find where the game was, and with him went a young man, the son of a chief. For many days they travelled over the prairies. They could see no game; roots and berries were their only food. One day they climbed to the crest of a high ridge, and as they looked off over the country they saw far away by a stream a lonely lodge.

"Who can it be?" asked the young man. "Who camps there alone, far from friends?"

"That," said Napi, "is he who has hidden all the animals from the people. He has a wife and a little son." Then they went down near to the lodge and Napi told the young man what to do. Napi changed himself into a little dog, and he said, "This is I." The young man changed himself into a root digger and he said, "This is I." Pretty soon the little boy, who was playing about near the lodge, found the dog and carried it to his father, saying, "See what a pretty little dog I have found."

The father said, "That is not a dog; throw it away!" The little boy cried, but his father made him take the dog out of the lodge. Then the boy found the root digger, and again picking up the dog, he carried both into the lodge, saying, "Look, mother; see what a pretty root digger I have found."

"Throw them away," said his father; "throw them both away. That is not a root digger; that is not a dog."

"I want that root digger," said the woman. "Let our son have the little dog."

35

"Let it be so, then," replied the husband; "but remember that if trouble comes, it is you who have brought it on yourself and on our son."

Soon after this the woman and her son went off to pick berries, and when they were out of sight the man went out and killed a buffalo cow and brought the meat into the lodge and covered it up. He took the bones and the skin and threw them in the water. When his wife came back he gave her some of the meat to roast, and while they were eating, the little boy fed the dog three times, and when he offered it more the father took the meat away.

In the night, when all were sleeping, Napi and the young man arose in their right shapes and ate some of the meat.

"You were right," said the young man. "This is surely the person who has hidden the buffalo."

"Wait," said Napi; and when they had finished eating they changed themselves again into the root digger and the dog.

Next morning the wife and the little boy went out to dig roots, and the woman took the root digger with her, while the dog followed the little boy.

As they travelled along looking for roots, they passed near a cave, and at its mouth stood a buffalo cow. The dog ran into the cave, and the root digger, slipping from the woman's hand, followed, gliding along over the ground like a snake. In this cave were found all the buffalo and the other game. They began to drive them out, and soon the prairie was covered with buffalo, antelope, and deer. Never before were so many seen.

Soon the man came running up, and he said to his wife, "Who is driving out my animals?" The woman replied, "The dog and the root digger are in there now."

"Did I not tell you," said her husband, "that those were not what they looked like. See now the trouble that you have brought upon us!" He put an arrow on his string and waited for them to come out, but they were cunning, and when the last animal, a big bull, was starting out the stick grasped him by the long hair under the neck and coiled up in it, and the dog held on by the hair underneath until they were far out on the prairie, when they changed into their true shapes and drove the buffalo toward the camp.

When the people saw the buffalo coming they led a big band of them to the piskun, but just as the leaders were about to jump over the cliff a raven came and flapped its wings in front of them and croaked, and they turned off and ran down another way. Every time a herd of buffalo was brought near to the piskun this raven frightened them away. Then Napi knew that the raven was the person who had kept the buffalo hidden.

Napi went down to the river and changed himself into a beaver and lay stretched out on a sandbar, as if dead. The raven was very hungry and flew down and began to pick at the beaver. Then Napi caught it by the legs and ran with it to the camp, and all the chiefs were called together to decide what should be done with the bird. Some said, "Let us kill it," but Napi said, "No, I will punish it," and he tied it up over the lodge, right in the smoke hole.

As the days went by the raven grew thin and weak and its eyes were blinded by the thick smoke, and it cried continually to Napi asking him to pity it. One day Napi untied the bird and told it to take its right shape, and then said, "Why have you tried to fool Napi? Look at me. I cannot die. Look at me. Of all peoples and tribes I am the chief. I cannot die. I made the mountains; they are standing yet. I made the prairies and the rocks; you see them yet.

"Go home now to your wife and your child, and when you are hungry hunt like any one else. If you do not, you shall die."

THE CAMP OF THE GHOSTS

THERE was once a man who loved his wife dearly. After they had been married for a time they had a little boy. Some time after that the woman grew sick and did not get well. She was sick for a long time. The young man loved his wife so much that he did not wish to take a second woman. The woman grew worse and worse. Doctoring did not seem to do her any good. At last she died.

For a few days after this, the man used to take his baby on his back and travel out away from the camp, walking over the hills, crying and mourning. He felt badly, and he did not know what to do.

After a time he said to the little child, "My little boy, you will have to go and live with your grandmother. I shall go away and try to find your mother and bring her back."

He took the baby to his mother's lodge and asked her to take care of it and left it with her. Then he started away, not knowing where he was going nor what he should do.

When he left the camp, he travelled toward the Sand Hills. On the fourth night of his journeying he had a dream. He dreamed that he went into a little lodge in which was an old woman. This old woman said to him, "Why are you here, my son?"

The young man replied, "I am mourning day and night, crying all the while. My little son, who is the only one left me, also mourns."

"Well," asked the old woman, "for whom are you mourning?"

The young man answered, "I am mourning for my wife. She died some time ago. I am looking for her."

"Oh, I saw her," said the old woman; "she passed this way. I myself have no great power to help you, but over by that far butte beyond, lives another old woman. Go to her and she will give you power to continue your journey. You could not reach the place you are seeking without help. Beyond the next butte from her lodge you will find the camp of the ghosts."

The next morning the young man awoke and went on toward the next butte. It took him a long summer's day to get there, but he found there no lodge, so he lay down and slept. Again he dreamed. In his dream he saw a little lodge, and saw an old woman come to the door and heard her call to him. He went into the lodge, and she spoke to him.

"My son, you are very unhappy. I know why you have come this way. You are looking for your wife who is now in the ghost country. It is a very hard thing for you to get there. You may not be able to get your wife back, but I have great power and I will do for you all that I can. If you act as I advise, you may succeed."

Other wise words she spoke to him, telling him what he should do; also she gave him a bundle of mysterious things which would help him on his journey.

She went on to say, "You stay here for a time and I will go over there to the ghosts'

camp and try to bring back some of your relations who are there. If it is possible for me to
bring them back, you may return there with
them, but on the way you must shut your eyes.
If you should open them and look about you,
you would die. Then you would never come
back. When you come to the camp you will
pass by a big lodge and they will ask you, 'Where
are you going and who told you to come here?'
You must answer, 'My grandmother, who is
standing out here with me, told me to come.'
They will try to scare you; they will make fearful noises and you will see strange and terrible
things, but do not be afraid."

The old woman went away, and after a time
came back with one of the man's relations.
He went with this relation to the ghosts' camp.
When they came to the large lodge some one
called out and asked the man what he was
doing there, and he answered as the old woman
had told him. As he passed on through the
camp the ghosts tried to frighten him with
many fearful sights and sounds, but he kept
up a strong heart.

43

Presently he came to another lodge, and the man who owned it came out and spoke to him, asking where he was going. The young man said, "I am looking for my dead wife. I mourn for her so much that I cannot rest. My little boy too keeps crying for his mother. They have offered to give me other wives, but I do not want them. I want the one for whom I am searching."

The ghost said, "It is a fearful thing that you have come here; it is very likely that you will never go away. Never before has there been a person here."

The ghost asked him to come into his lodge, and he entered.

This chief ghost said to him, "You shall stay here for four nights and you shall see your wife, but you must be very careful or you will never go back. You will die here in this very place."

Then the chief ghost walked out of the lodge and shouted out for a feast, inviting the man's father-in-law and other relations who were in the camp to come and eat, saying, "Your son-

44

in-law invites you to a feast," as if he meant that the son-in-law had died and become a ghost and arrived at the camp of the ghosts.

Now when these invited ghosts had reached the lodge they did not like to go in. They said to each other, "There is a person here"; it seemed as if they did not like the smell of a human being. The chief ghost burned sweet pine on the fire, which took away this smell, and then the ghosts came in and sat down.

The chief ghost said to them, "Now pity this son-in-law of yours. He is looking for his wife. Neither the great distance that he has come nor the fearful sights that he has seen here have weakened his heart. You can see how tender-hearted he is. He not only mourns because he has lost his wife, but he mourns because his little boy is now alone, with no mother; so pity him and give him back his wife."

The ghosts talked among themselves, and one of them said to the man, "Yes; you shall stay here for four nights, and then we will give you a medicine pipe—the Worm Pipe—and we will give you back your wife and you may return to your home."

Now, after the third night the chief ghost called together all the people, and they came, and with them came the man's wife. One of the ghosts was beating a drum, and following him was another who carried the Worm Pipe, which they gave to him.

Then the chief ghost said, "Now be very careful; to-morrow you and your wife will start on your journey homeward. Your wife will carry the medicine pipe and for four days some of your relations will go along with you. During this time you must keep your eyes shut; do not open them, or you will return here and be a ghost forever. Your wife is not now a person. But in the middle of the fourth day you will be told to look, and when you have opened your eyes you will see that your wife has become a person, and that your ghost relations have disappeared."

Before the man went away his father-in-law spoke to him and said, "When you get near home you must not go at once into the camp.

Let some of your relations know that you have come, and ask them to build a sweat-house for you. Go into that sweat-house and wash your body thoroughly, leaving no part of it, however small, uncleansed. If you fail in this, you will die. There is something about the ghosts that it is difficult to remove. It can only be removed by a thorough sweat. Take care now that you do what I tell you. Do not whip your wife, nor strike her with a knife, nor hit her with fire. If you do, she will vanish before your eyes and return here."

They left the ghost country to go home, and on the fourth day the wife said to her husband, "Open your eyes." He looked about him and saw that those who had been with them had disappeared, and he found that they were standing in front of the old woman's lodge by the butte. She came out of her lodge and said to them, "Stop; give me back those mysterious medicines of mine, whose power helped you to do what you wished." The man returned them to her, and then once more became really a living person.

When they drew near to the camp the woman went on ahead and sat down on a butte. Then some curious persons came out to see who this might be. As they approached the woman called out to them, "Do not come any nearer. Go and tell my mother and my relations to put up a lodge for us a little way from the camp, and near by it build a sweat-house." When this had been done the man and his wife went in and took a thorough sweat, and then they went into the lodge and burned sweet grass and purified their clothing and the Worm Pipe. Then their relations and friends came in to see them. The man told them where he had been and how he had managed to get his wife back, and that the pipe hanging over the doorway was a medicine pipe—the Worm Pipe—presented to him by his ghost father-in-law.

That is how the people came to possess the Worm Pipe. That pipe belongs to the band of Piegans known as the Worm People.

Not long after this, once in the night, this man told his wife to do something, and when she did not begin at once he picked up a brand

48

from the fire and raised it—not that he intended to strike her with it, but he made as if he would —when all at once she vanished and was never seen again.

THE BUFFALO STONE

A SMALL stone, which is often a fossil shell, or sometimes only a queer shaped piece of flint, is called by the Blackfeet I-nĭs′kĭm, the buffalo stone. This stone has great power, and gives its owner good luck in bringing the buffalo close, so that they may be killed. The stone is found on the prairie, and any one who finds one is thought to be very lucky. Sometimes a man who is going along on the prairie will hear a queer faint chirp, such as a little bird might make. He knows this sound is made by a buffalo stone. He stops and searches for it on the ground, and if he cannot find it, marks the place and comes back next day to look for it again. If it is found, he and all his family are glad. The Blackfeet tell a story about how the first buffalo stone was found.

Long ago, one winter, the buffalo disappeared. The snow was deep, so deep that the people

could not move in search of the buffalo; so
the hunters went as far as they could up and
down the river-bottoms and in the ravines, and
killed deer and elk and other small game, and
when these were all killed or driven away the
people began to starve.

One day a young married man killed a prairie
rabbit. He ran home as fast as he could, and
told one of his wives to hurry and get a skin of
water to cook it. She started down to the river
for water, and as she was going along she heard
a beautiful song. She looked all about, but
could see no one who was singing.

The song seemed to come from a big cotton-
wood tree near the trail leading down to the
water. As she looked closely at this tree she
saw a queer stone jammed in a fork where the
tree was split, and with it a few hairs from a
buffalo which had rubbed against the tree.
The woman was frightened and dared not pass
the tree. Soon the singing stopped and the
I-nĭs′kĭm said to the woman, "Take me to your
lodge, and when it is dark call in the people and
teach them the song you have just heard. Pray,

too, that you may not starve, and that the buffalo may come back. Do this, and when day
comes your hearts will be glad."

The woman went on and got the water, and
when she came back she took the stone and gave
it to her husband, telling him about the song and
what the stone had said.

As soon as it was dark, the man called the
chiefs and old men to his lodge, and his wife
taught them the song that she had heard. They
prayed too, as the stone had said should be done.
Before long they heard far off a noise coming.
It was the tramp of a great herd of buffalo.
Then they knew that the stone was powerful,
and since that time the people have taken care
of it and have prayed to it.

HOW THE THUNDER PIPE CAME

YOU have heard the Thunder, for he is everywhere. He roars in the mountains, and far out on the prairie is heard his crashing. He strikes the high rocks, and they fall to pieces; a tree, and it is broken in slivers; the people, and they die. He is bad. He does not like the high cliff, the standing tree, or living man. He likes to strike and crush them to the ground. Of all things he is the most powerful. He cannot be resisted. But I have not told you the worst thing about him. Sometimes he takes away women.

Long ago, almost in the beginning, a man and his wife were sitting in their lodge when Thunder came and struck them. The man was not killed. At first he lay as if dead, but after a time he lived again, and, standing up, looked about him. He did not see his wife.

53

"Oh," he thought, "she has gone to get wood or water," and he sat down again. But when night came he went out of the lodge and asked the people about her. No one had seen her. He looked all through the camp, but could not find her. Then he knew that the Thunder had taken her away, and he went out on the hills and mourned. All night he sat there, trying to think what he might do to get back his wife.

When morning came he rose and wandered away, and whenever he met any of the animals he asked if they could tell him where the Thunder lived. The animals laughed, and most of them would not answer.

The Wolf said to him, "Do you think that we would look for the home of the only one we fear? He is our only danger. From all other enemies we can run away, but from him no one can run. He strikes and there we lie. Turn back; go home. Do not look for the place of that dreadful one."

The man kept on and travelled a long distance. At last, after many days, he came to a lodge—a strange lodge, for it was made of stone. Just like any other lodge it looked, only it was made of stone. This was the home of the Raven chief. The man entered.

"Welcome, friend," said the chief of the Ravens; "sit down there," and he pointed to a place. Soon food was placed before the poor man.

When he had finished eating, the Raven chief asked, "Why have you come here?"

"Thunder has stolen my wife," the man answered. "I am looking for his dwelling-place that I may find her."

"Are you brave enough to enter the lodge of that dreadful person?" asked the Raven. "He lives near here. His lodge is of stone like this one, and hanging in it are eyes—the eyes of those he has killed or taken away. He has taken out their eyes and hung them in his lodge. Now, then! Dare you enter there?"

"No," answered the man, "I am afraid. Who could look at such dreadful things and live?"

"No man can," said the Raven; "there is

only one old Thunder fears; there is but one he
cannot kill. It is we. It is the Ravens. Now
I will give you some medicine, and he shall not
harm you. You shall enter there and try to
find among those eyes your wife's, and if you
find them tell the Thunder why you came and
make him give them to you. Here, now, is a
raven's wing. Point this at him and he will
be afraid and start back; but if that should
fail, take this arrow. Its shaft is made of elk
horn. Take this, I say, and shoot it through
the lodge."

"Why make a fool of me?" the poor man
asked. "My heart is sad. I am crying." He
covered his head with his robe and wept.

"Oh," said the Raven, "you do not believe
me. Come outside, come outside, and I will
make you believe."

When they stood outside the Raven asked,
"Is the home of your people far?"

"A great distance," said the man.

"Can you tell how many days you have travelled?"

"No," he replied, "my heart was sad; I did

not count the days. Since I left, the berries have grown and ripened."

"Can you see your camp from here?" asked the Raven.

The man did not answer. Then the Raven rubbed some medicine on his eyes and said, "Look!" The man looked and saw the camp. It was near. He saw the people; he saw the smoke rising from the lodges; he saw the painting on some of the lodges.

"Now you will believe," said the Raven. "Take, then, the arrow and the wing, and go and get your wife." The man took these things and went to the Thunder's lodge. He entered and sat down by the doorway.

The Thunder sat at the back of the lodge and looked at him with awful eyes. The man looked above and saw hanging there many pairs of eyes. Among them were those of his wife.

"Why have you come?" said the Thunder in a dreadful voice.

"I seek my wife," said the man, "whom you have stolen. There hang her eyes."

57

"No man may enter my lodge and live," said the Thunder, and he rose to strike him. Then the man pointed the raven wing at the Thunder, and he fell back on his bed and shivered; but soon he recovered and rose again, and then the man fitted the elk-horn arrow to his bow and shot it through the lodge of stone. Right through that stone it pierced a hole and let the sunlight in.

"Wait," said the Thunder; "stop. You are the stronger, you have the greater medicine. You shall have your wife. Take down her eyes."

The man cut the string that held the eyes, and his wife stood beside him.

"Now," said the Thunder, "you know me. I have great power. In summer I live here; but when winter comes I go far south. I go south with the birds. Here is my pipe. It has strong power. Take it and keep it. After this, when first I come in the spring you shall fill this pipe and light it, and you shall smoke it and pray to me; you and the people. I bring the rain which makes the berries large and ripe.

58

I bring the rain which makes all things grow, and for this you shall pray to me; you and all the people."

Thus the people got their first medicine pipe. It was long ago.

COLD MAKER'S MEDICINE

THE last lodge had been set up in the Black-feet winter camp. Evening was closing over the travel-tired people. The sun had dropped beyond the hills not far away. Women were bringing water from the river at the edge of the great circle. Men gathered in quiet groups, weary after the long march of the day. Children called sleepily to each other, and the dogs sniffed about in well-fed content.

Lone Feather wrapped his robe more closely around him and walked slowly from his lodge door and from the camp, off toward the north. He was thinking of many things, and hardly noticed where he was going. Presently as he walked, he heard the sound of persons talking. He stopped to listen. The sound came from a lodge made of stone, close by the river. Quietly he went toward the lodge and saw a thin blue line of smoke coming from the top.

As he approached, an old woman, bent with age and crippled, came from the lodge door and looked at him.

"Will you come into my lodge?" she said, greeting him.

Lone Feather looked at her for a moment in silence. She spoke again. He could not understand her speech, for she belonged to another tribe. By signs she made him know that she wished him to come into her lodge and rest. Lone Feather entered.

Far back from the door crouched two big grizzly bears. She made signs to show that the bears were friendly, and Lone Feather sat down near the door. She stirred the fire, and as she put on fresh wood the sparks flew up toward the smoke hole, which was opened only a little way.

By signs she told him she would go out and open the smoke hole wider, so that the fire might burn more brightly. She was gone for some time, and Lone Feather sat looking into the fire, still thinking of many things, when the air became thick with smoke. He looked up and saw that the smoke hole was closed. He sprang up and went to the door, but the door covering was down. He raised it, and as he put his head out the old woman hit him with a large stone club and he was dead.

Before his spirit started for the Sand Hills he saw that with a large knife she cut up his body and put the pieces into a pot. Soon they were well cooked and the old woman and the two bears feasted on his flesh.

They threw his bones out of the door, where they fell among many others like them. The ground was strewn with the bones of the persons she had trapped and killed.

Day by day other persons disappeared from the winter camp, and more and more bones whitened on the ground outside the stone lodge on the river bank.

As Cold Maker was bringing the snow to the Blackfeet winter camp, he passed the Sand Hills. Lone Feather and other ghosts from the Blackfeet tribe were telling each other how the old woman had sent them there. Cold Maker heard their stories and he was angry.

When he reached the camp he went to the

lodge of Broken Bow—a brave young man, but very poor.

He shivered when Cold Maker entered his lodge and drew his ragged robe about him. They were close friends.

"Would you like to have a new robe?" asked Cold Maker.

"Yes," said Broken Bow.

"Come with me. You may kill two grizzly bears," said Cold Maker.

"My bow is broken. I cannot," said Broken Bow sadly.

"I will help you. Bring only a knife."

Together they went from the lodges toward the north. The sun was already hidden behind the nearby hills.

After they had travelled some distance they heard the sound of voices. They listened. Two bears were complaining that they wanted meat. A woman told them they must wait. The men saw the line of thin blue smoke rising from the top of the lodge of stone. All about whitening bones covered the ground. They went nearer.

Soon an old woman, bent with age and crip-

pled, came from the door and smiled as she saw
the two persons coming.

"Come in and rest," she said. Broken Bow
did not understand her language, but Cold
Maker, who understands all tribes, said, "We
are cold. Will you let us sit by your fire?"

The old woman smiled again.

"You are welcome," she said; "come in. Do
not fear my bears. They are friendly. They
will not harm you." The two friends entered
the lodge, where a smouldering fire sent a feeble
smoke up to the smoke hole, that was partly
open. She put fresh wood on the fire and said,
"I will open the smoke hole wider," and went
out, dropping the door covering as she went.

Then she closed the smoke hole. The smoke
began to fill the top of the lodge. It settled
lower and lower. Broken Bow was afraid.

"Give me your pipe," said Cold Maker.

Broken Bow filled his pipe and handed it to
him. He lighted it by a brand from the fire,
and sent great puffs of smoke curling upward.
This smoke met the other smoke and stopped it.
It could not descend any lower.

Broken Bow saw the wonderful medicine of his friend. He was no longer afraid, but wondered what Cold Maker would do next. The grizzly bears growled low.

The old woman outside called to them, "Friends, is it smoking in there now?"

"Not a bit," replied Cold Maker. "We are very comfortable."

She waited. They did not come out. She stood near the door. Her stone club was ready. She grew impatient. She wondered what had gone wrong with her plans. The two friends were silent. She looked at the smoke hole, but it was closed securely. She lifted the door covering to see if the friends within had died. They sat perfectly still. She entered to look more closely, and as soon as she was fairly inside Cold Maker and Broken Bow rushed out and dropped the door covering. Before she could move they piled great heaps of stone in the door-way. The bears growled. She called for help. Cold Maker and Broken Bow went on down the river.

Then Cold Maker took from a little sack a

few white eagle-down feathers. He blew them from him. At once a fierce storm blew across the valley. The bitter cold froze the water, but only in this one place. It dammed the stream with fast forming ice. The water rose higher and higher. It spread out over the banks. Cold Maker and Broken Bow went far off on the hills and watched it. Little by little it rose. It reached the stone lodge. The bears roared. The woman screamed. The water reached the top and covered the lodge from sight. All sound ceased. A moment more, and the water was quiet. Once more Cold Maker blew from him a few white eagle-down feathers. The storm subsided. It became warm again. The ice melted. The water retreated to its channel.

Cold Maker and Broken Bow went to the stone lodge. The woman was lying beside the pot. The grizzly bears were close to the stones which blocked the door-way.

Cold Maker said, "Here is your new robe," and Broken Bow took from the bears their thick, warm skins.

On his way home Cold Maker again passed the Sand Hills. Entering the country was an old woman bent with age and crippled.

He hurried on.

THE ALL COMRADES SOCIETIES

IN the Blackfeet tribe was an association known as the All Comrades. This was made up of a dozen secret societies graded according to age, the members of the younger societies passing, after a few years, into the older ones. This association was in part benevolent and helpful and in part to encourage bravery in war, but its main purpose was to see that the orders of the chiefs were carried out, and to punish offences against the tribe at large. There are stories which explain how these societies came to be instituted, and this one tells how the Society of Bulls began.

THE BULLS SOCIETY

IT was long, long ago, very far back, that this happened. In those days the people used to kill the buffalo by driving them over a steep place near the river, down which they fell into a great pen built at the foot of the cliff, where the buffalo that had not been killed by the fall were shot with arrows by the men. Then the people went into the pen and skinned the buffalo and cut them up and carried the meat away to their camp. This pen they called piskun.

In those days the people had built a great piskun with high, strong walls. No buffalo could jump over it; not even if a great crowd of them ran against it, could they push it down.

The young men kept going out, as they always did, to try to bring the buffalo to the edge of the cliff, but somehow they would not jump over into the piskun. When they had come almost to the edge, they would turn off to one side or the other and run down the sloping hills and away over the prairie. So the people could get no food, and they began to be hungry, and at last to starve.

Early one morning a young woman, the daughter of a brave man, was going from her lodge down to the stream to get water, and as she went along she saw a herd of buffalo feeding on the prairie, close to the edge of the cliff above the great piskun.

"Oh," she called out, "if you will only jump off into the piskun I will marry one of you." She did not mean this, but said it just in fun, and as soon as she had said it, she wondered greatly when she saw the buffalo come jumping over the edge, falling down the cliff.

A moment later a big bull jumped high over the wall of the piskun and came toward her, and now truly she was frightened.

"Come," he said, taking hold of her arm.

"No, no," she answered, trying to pull herself away.

"But you said if the buffalo would only jump over, you would marry one of them. Look, the piskun is full."

She did not answer, and without saying anything more he led her up over the bluff and out on the prairie.

After the people had finished killing the buffalo and cutting up the meat, they missed this young woman. No one knew where she had gone, and her relations were frightened and very sad because they could not find her. So her father took his bow and quiver and put them on his back and said, "I will go and find her"; and he climbed the bluff and set out over the prairie.

He travelled some distance, but saw nothing of his daughter. The sun was hot, and at length he came to a buffalo wallow in which some water was standing, and drank and sat down to rest. A little way off on the prairie he saw a herd of buffalo. As the man sat there by the wallow, trying to think what he might do to find his daughter, a magpie came up and alighted on the ground near him. The man spoke to it, saying, "Măm-ĭ-ăt′sĭ-kĭmĭ—Magpie —you are a beautiful bird; help me, for I am very unhappy. As you travel about over the prairie, look everywhere, and if you see my daughter say to her, 'Your father is waiting by the wallow.'"

Soon the magpie flew away, and as he passed near the herd of buffalo he saw the young woman there, and alighting on the ground near her, he began to pick at things, turning his head this way and that, and seeming to look for food.

When he was close to the girl he said to her, "Your father is waiting by the wallow."

"Sh-h-h! Sh-h-h!" replied the girl in a whisper, looking about her very much frightened, for her bull husband was sleeping close by. "Do not speak so loud. Go back and tell him to wait."

"Your daughter is over there with the buffalo. She says 'Wait,'" said the magpie when he had flown back to the poor father.

After a little time the bull awoke and said to his wife, "Go and bring me some water." Then the woman was glad, and she took a horn from her husband's head and went to the wallow for water.

"Oh, why did you come?" she said to her father. "They will surely kill you."

"I came to take my daughter back to my lodge. Come, let us go."

"No," said the girl, "not now. They will surely chase us and kill us. Wait until he sleeps again and I will try to get away." Then she filled the horn with water and went back to the buffalo.

Her husband drank a swallow of the water, and when he took the horn it made a noise. "Ah," he said, as he looked about, "a person is somewhere close by."

"No one," replied the girl, but her heart stood still. The bull drank again. Then he stood up on his feet and moaned and grunted, "M-m-ah-oo! Bu-u-u!" Fearful was the sound. Up rose the other bulls, raised their tails in the air, tossed their heads and bellowed back to him. Then they pawed the earth, thrust their horns into it, rushed here and there, and presently, coming to the wallow, found there the poor man. They rushed over him, trampling him with their great hoofs, thrust their horns into his body and tore him to pieces, and trampled him again. Soon not even a piece of his body could be seen—only the wet earth cut up by their hoofs.

Then his daughter mourned in sorrow. *"Oh! Ah! Ni-nah-ah! Oh! Ah! Ni-nah-ah!"*—Ah, my father, my father.

"Ah," said her bull husband; "now you understand how it is that we feel. You mourn for your father; but we have seen our fathers, mothers, and many of our relations fall over the high cliffs, to be killed for food by your people. But now I will pity you, I will give you one chance. If you can bring your father to life, you and he may go back to your camp."

Then said the woman, "Ah, magpie, pity me, help me; for now I need help. Look in the trampled mud of the wallow and see if you can find even a little piece of my father's body and bring it to me."

Swiftly the magpie flew to the wallow, and alighting there, walked all about, looking in every hole and even tearing up the mud with his sharp beak. Presently he uncovered something white, and as he picked the mud from about it, he saw it was a bone, and pulling hard, he dragged it from the mud—the joint of a man's backbone. Then gladly he flew back with it to the woman.

The girl put the bone on the ground and covered it with her robe and began to sing. After she had sung she took the robe away, and there under it lay her father's body, as if he had just

74

died. Once again she covered the body with the robe and sang, and this time when she took the robe away the body was breathing. A third time she covered the body with the robe and sang, and when she again took away the robe, the body moved its arms and legs a little. A fourth time she covered it and sang, and when she took away the robe her father stood up.

The buffalo were surprised and the magpie was glad, and flew about making a great noise.

"Now this day we have seen a strange thing," said her bull husband. "The people's medicine is strong. He whom we trampled to death, whom our hoofs cut to pieces and mixed all up with the soil, is alive again. Now you shall go to your home, but before you go we will teach you our dance and our song. Do not forget them."

The buffalo showed the man and his daughter their dance and taught them the songs, and then the bull said to them, "Now you are to go back to your home, but do not forget what you have seen. Teach the people this dance and these songs, and while they are dancing it let them wear a bull's head and a robe. Those who are to be of the Bulls Society shall wear them."

When the poor man returned with his daughter, all the people were glad. Then after a time he called a council of the chiefs and told them the things that had happened. The chiefs chose certain young men to be Bulls, and the man taught them the dance and the song, and told them everything that they should do.

So began the Bull Society.

THE OTHER SOCIETIES

For a long time the buffalo had not been seen. Every one was hungry, for the hunters could find no food for the people.

A certain man, who had two wives, a daughter, and two sons, as he saw what a hard time they were having, said, "I shall not stop here to die. To-morrow we will move toward the mountains, where we may kill elk and deer and sheep and antelope, or, if not these, at least we shall find beaver and birds, and can get them. In this way we shall have food to eat and shall live."

Next morning they caught their dogs and harnessed them to the travois and took their loads on their backs and set out. It was still winter, and they travelled slowly. Besides, they were weak from hunger and could go only a short distance in a day. The fourth night came, and they sat in their lodge, tired and hungry. No one spoke, for people who are hungry do not care to talk. Suddenly, outside, the dogs began to bark, and soon the door was pushed aside and a young man entered.

"Welcome," said the man, and he motioned to a place where the stranger should sit.

Now during this day there had been blowing a warm wind which had melted the snow, so that the prairie was covered with water, yet this young man's moccasins and leggings were dry. They saw this, and were frightened. They sat there for a long time, saying nothing.

Then the young man spoke and asked, "Why is this? Why do you not give me food?"

"Ah," replied the father, "you see here people who are truly poor. We have no food. For many days the buffalo did not come in sight, and we looked for deer and other animals which people eat, and when these had all been killed we began to starve. Then I said, 'We will not stay here to die from hunger,' and we set out for the mountains. This is the fourth night of our travels."

"Ah," said the young man, "then your travels are ended. You need go no farther. Close by here is our piskun. Many buffalo have been run in, and our parfleches are filled with dried meat. Wait a little; I will go and bring you some," and he went out.

As soon as he had gone they began to talk about this strange person. They were afraid of him and did not know what to do. The children began to cry, and the women tried to quiet them. Presently the young man came back, bringing some meat.

"There is food," said he, as he put it down by the woman. "Now to-morrow move your camp over to our lodges. Do not fear anything. No matter what strange things you may see, do not fear. All will be your friends. Yet about one thing I must warn you. In this you should

78

be careful. If you should find an arrow lying about anywhere, in the piskun or outside, do not touch it, neither you nor your wives nor your children." When he had said this he went out.

The father took his pipe and filled it, and smoked and prayed to all the powers, saying, "Hear now, Sun; listen, Above People; listen, Underwater People; now you have taken pity; now you have given us food. We are going to those mysterious ones who walk through water with dry moccasins. Protect us among these to-be-feared people. Let us live. Man, woman, and child, give us long life."

Now from the fire again arose the smell of roasting meat. The children ate and played. Those who so long had been silent now talked and laughed.

Early in the morning, as soon as the sun had risen, they took down their lodge and packed their dogs and started for the camp of the stranger. When they had come to where they could see it, they found it a wonderful place. There around the piskun, and stretching far up and down the valley, were pitched the lodges of the meat eaters. They could not see them all, but near by they saw the lodges of the Bear band, the Fox band, and the Raven band. The father of the young man who had visited them and given them meat was the chief of the Wolf band, and by that band they pitched their lodge. Truly that was a happy place. Food was plenty. All day long people were shouting out for feasts, and everywhere was heard the sound of drumming and singing and dancing.

The newly come people went to the piskun for meat, and there one of the children saw an arrow lying on the ground. It was a beautiful arrow, the stone point long, slender, and sharp, the shaft round and straight. The boy remembered what had been said and he looked around fearfully, but everywhere the people were busy. No one was looking. He picked up the arrow and put it under his robe.

Then there rose a terrible sound. All the animals howled and growled and rushed toward him, but the chief Wolf got to him first, and holding up his hand said, "Wait. He is young

80

and not yet of good sense. We will let him go this time." They did nothing to him.

When night came some one shouted out, calling people to a feast and saying, "Listen, listen, Wolf, you are to eat; enter with your friend."

"We are invited," said the chief Wolf to his new friend, and together they went to the lodge from which the call came.

Within the lodge the fire burned brightly, and seated around it were many men, the old and wise of the Raven band. On the lodge lining, hanging behind the seats, were the paintings of many great deeds. Food was placed before the guests—pemican and berries and dried back fat—and after they had eaten the pipe was lighted and passed around the circle. Then the Raven chief spoke and said, "Now, Wolf, I am going to give our new friend a present. What do you think of that?"

"It shall be as you say," replied the Wolf; "our new friend will be glad."

From a long parfleche sack the Raven chief took a slender stick, beautifully ornamented

with many-colored feathers. To the end of the
stick was tied the skin of a raven—head, wings,
feet, and tail.

"We," said the Raven chief, "are those who
carry the raven (Măs-to-pāh'-tă-kĭks). Of all
the fliers, of all the birds, what one is so smart
as the raven? None. The raven's eyes are
sharp, his wings are strong. He is a great
hunter and never hungry. Far off on the
prairie he sees his food, or if it is deep hidden
in the forest it does not escape him. This is
our song and our dance."

When he had finished singing and dancing
he placed the stick in the sack and gave it to
the man and said, "Take it with you, and when
you have returned to your people you shall
say, 'Now there are already the Bulls, and he
who is the Raven chief said, "There shall be more.
There shall be the All Friends (Ĭkŭn-ŭh'-
kāh-tsĭ), so that the people may live, and of the
All Friends shall be the Raven Bearers."'" You
shall call a council of the chiefs and wise old
men, and they shall choose the persons who are
to belong to the society. Teach them the song

and the dance, and give them the medicine. It shall be theirs forever."

Soon they heard another person shouting out the feast call, and, going, they entered the lodge of the chief of the Kit-Foxes (Sĭn'-o-pah). Here, too, old men had gathered. After they had eaten of the food set before them, the chief said, "Those among whom you have just come are generous. They do not look carefully at the things they have, but give to the stranger and pity the poor. The kit-fox is a little animal, but what one is smarter? None. His hair is like the dead grass of the prairie; his eyes are keen; his feet make no noise when he walks; his brain is cunning. His ears receive the far-off sound. Here is our medicine. Take it." He gave the man the stick. It was long, crooked at one end, wound with fur, and tied here and there with eagle feathers. At the end was a kit-fox skin. Again the chief spoke and said, "Listen to our song. Do not forget it, and the dance, too, you must remember. When you reach home teach them to the people." He sang and danced. Then presently his guests departed.

Again they heard the feast shout, and he who called was the chief of the Bear society. After they had eaten and smoked the chief said,

"What is your opinion, friend Wolf? Shall we give our new friend a present?"

"It shall be as you say," replied the Wolf. "It is yours to give."

Then spoke the Bear, saying, "There are many animals and some of them are powerful; but the bear is the strongest and greatest of all. He fears nothing and is always ready to fight."

Then he put on a necklace of bear claws, a band of bear fur about his head, and a belt of bear fur, and sang and danced. When he had finished he gave the things he had worn to the man and said, "Teach the people our song and our dance, and give them this medicine. It is powerful."

It was very late. The Seven Stars had come to the middle of the night, yet again they heard the feast shout from the far end of the camp. In this lodge the men were painted with streaks of red, and their hair was all pushed to one side.

After the feast the chief said, "We are different from all others here. We are called the Braves (Mŭt'-sĭks). We know not fear; we are death. Even if our enemies are as many as the grass we do not turn away, but fight and conquer. Bows are good weapons, lances are better; but our weapon is the knife."

Then the chief sang and danced, and afterward he gave the Wolf chief's friend the medicine. It was a long knife and many scalps were tied on the handle. "This," said he, "is for the All Friends."

To one more lodge they were called that night and the lodge owner taught the man his song and dance, and gave him his medicine. Then the Wolf chief and his friend went home and slept.

Early next day the Blackfeet women began to take down the lodge and to get ready to move their camp. Many women came and made them presents of food, dried meat, pemican, and berries. They were given so much that they could not take it all with them. It was long before they joined the main camp, for it had moved south, looking for buffalo.

When they reached the camp, as soon as the lodge was pitched, the man called all the chiefs to come and feast with him, and told them what he had seen, and showed them the different medicines. Then the chiefs chose certain young men to belong to the different societies, and this man taught them the songs and dances, and gave its medicine to each society.

THE FIRST MEDICINE LODGE

THE chief god of the Blackfeet is the Sun. He made the world and rules it, and to him the people pray. One of his names is Napi —old man; but there is another Napi who is very different from the Sun, and instead of being great, wise, and wonderful, is foolish, mean, and contemptible. We shall hear about him further on.

Every year in summer, about the time the berries ripen, the Blackfeet used to hold the great festival and sacrifice which we call the ceremony of the Medicine Lodge. This was a time of happy meetings, of feasting, of giving presents; but besides this rejoicing, those men who wished to have good-luck in whatever they might undertake tried to prove their prayers sincere by sacrificing their bodies, torturing themselves in ways that caused great suffering.

In ancient times, as we are told in books of history, things like that used to happen among many peoples all over the world.

It was the law that the building of the Medicine Lodge must always be pledged by a good woman. If a woman had a son or a husband away at war and feared that he was in danger, or if she had a child that was sick and might die, she might pray for the safety of the one she loved, and promise that if he returned or recovered she would build a Medicine Lodge. This pledge was made in a loud voice, publicly, in open air, so that all might know the promise had been made.

At the time appointed all the tribe came together and pitched their lodges in a great circle, and within this circle the Medicine Lodge was built. The ceremony lasted for four days and four nights, during which time the woman who had promised to make the Medicine Lodge neither ate nor drank, except once in sacrifice. Different stories are told of how the first Medicine Lodge came to be built. This is one of those stories:

THE FIRST MEDICINE LODGE

In the earliest times there was a man who had a very beautiful daughter. Many young men wished to marry her, but whenever she was asked she shook her head and said she did not wish to marry.

"Why is this?" said her father. "Some of these young men are rich, handsome, and brave."

"Why should I marry?" replied the girl. "My father and mother take care of me. Our lodge is good; the parfleches are never empty; there are plenty of tanned robes and soft furs for winter. Why trouble me, then?"

Soon after, the Raven Bearers held a dance. They all painted themselves nicely and wore their finest ornaments and each one tried to dance the best. Afterward some of them asked for this girl, but she said, "No." After that the Bulls, the Kit-Foxes, and others of the All Comrades held their dances, and many men who were rich and some great warriors asked this man for his daughter, but to every one she said, "No."

Then her father was angry, and he said, "Why is this? All the best men have asked for you, and still you say 'No.'" Then the girl said, "Father, listen to me. That Above Person, the Sun, said to me, 'Do not marry any of these men, for you belong to me. Listen to what I say, and you shall be happy and live to a great age.' And again he said to me, 'Take heed, you must not marry; you are mine.'"

"Ah!" replied her father; "it must always be as he says"; and they spoke no more about it.

There was a poor young man. He was very poor. His father, his mother, and all his relations were dead. He had no lodge, no wife to tan his robes or make his moccasins. His clothes were always old and worn. He had no home. To-day he stopped in one lodge; then to-morrow he ate and slept in another. Thus he lived. He had a good face, but on his cheek was a bad scar.

After they had held those dances, some of the young men met this poor Scarface, and they laughed at him and said, "Why do not you ask that girl to marry you? You are so rich and handsome."

Scarface did not laugh. He looked at them

and said, "I will do as you say; I will go and ask her."

All the young men thought this was funny; they laughed a good deal at Scarface as he was walking away.

Scarface went down by the river and waited there, near the place where the women went to get water. By and by the girl came there. Scarface spoke to her, and said, "Girl, stop; I want to speak with you. I do not wish to do anything secretly, but I speak to you here openly, where the Sun looks down and all may see."

"Speak, then," said the girl.

"I have seen the days," said Scarface. "I have seen how you have refused all those men, who are young and rich and brave. To-day some of these young men laughed and said to me, 'Why do not you ask her?' I am poor. I have no lodge, no food, no clothes, no robes. I have no relations. All of them have died. Yet now to-day I say to you, take pity. Be my wife."

The girl hid her face in her robe and brushed the ground with the point of her moccasin, back and forth, back and forth, for she was thinking.

After a time she spoke and said, "It is true I have refused all those rich young men; yet now a poor one asks me, and I am glad. I will be your wife, and my people will be glad. You are poor, but that does not matter. My father will give you dogs; my mother will make us a lodge; my relations will give us robes and furs; you will no longer be poor."

Then the young man was glad, and he started forward to kiss her, but she put out her hand and held him back, and said, "Wait; the Sun has spoken to me. He said I may not marry; that I belong to him; that if I listen to him I shall live to great age. So now I say, go to the Sun; say to him, 'She whom you spoke with has listened to your words; she has never done wrong, but now she wants to marry. I want her for my wife.' Ask him to take that scar from your face; that will be his sign, and I shall know he is pleased. But if he refuses, or if you cannot find his lodge, then do not return to me."

92

"Oh!" cried Scarface; "at first your words were good. I was glad. But now it is dark. My heart is dead. Where is that far-off lodge? Where is the trail that no one yet has travelled?"

"Take courage, take courage," said the girl softly, and she went on to her lodge.

Scarface was very unhappy. He did not know what to do. He sat down and covered his face with his robe, and tried to think. At length he stood up and went to an old woman who had been kind to him, and said to her, "Pity me. I am very poor. I am going away, on a long journey. Make me some moccasins."

"Where are you going—far from the camp?" asked the old woman.

"I do not know where I am going," he replied; "I am in trouble, but I cannot talk about it."

This old woman had a kind heart. She made him moccasins—seven pairs; and gave him also a sack of food—pemican, dried meat, and back fat.

All alone, and with a sad heart, Scarface climbed the bluff that overlooked the valley, and when he had reached the top, turned to look back at the camp. He wondered if he should ever see it again; if he should return to the girl and to the people.

"Pity me, O Sun!" he prayed; and turning away, he set off to look for the trail to the Sun's lodge.

For many days he went on. He crossed great prairies and followed up timbered rivers, and crossed the mountains. Every day his sack of food grew lighter, but as he went along he looked for berries and roots, and sometimes he killed an animal. These things gave him food.

One night he came to the home of a wolf. "Hah!" said the wolf; "what are you doing so far from your home?"

"I am looking for the place where the Sun lives," replied Scarface. "I have been sent to speak with him."

"I have travelled over much country," said the wolf; "I know all the prairies, the valleys, and the mountains; but I have never seen the Sun's home. But wait a moment. I know a person who is very wise, and who may be able to tell you the road. Ask the bear."

The next day Scarface went on again, stopping now and then to rest and to pick berries, and when night came he was at the bear's lodge.

"Where is your home?" asked the bear. "Why are you travelling so far alone?"

"Ah," replied the man, "I have come to you for help. Pity me. Because of what that girl said to me, I am looking for the Sun. I wish to ask him for her."

"I do not know where he lives," said the bear. "I have travelled by many rivers and I know the mountains, yet I have not seen his lodge. Farther on there is some one—that striped face—who knows a great deal; ask him."

When the young man got there, the badger was in his hole. But Scarface called to him, "Oh, cunning striped face! I wish to speak with you."

The badger put his head out of the hole and said, "What do you want, my brother?"

"I wish to find the Sun's home," said Scarface. "I wish to speak with him."

"I do not know where he lives," answered the badger. "I never travel very far. Over there in the timber is the wolverene. He is always travelling about, and knows many things. Perhaps he can tell you."

Scarface went over to the forest and looked all about for the wolverene, but could not see him; so he sat down on a log to rest. "Alas, alas!" he cried; "wolverene, take pity on me. My food is gone, my moccasins are worn out; I fear I shall die."

Some one close to him said, "What is it, my brother?" and looking around, he saw the wolverene sitting there.

"She whom I wish to marry belongs to the Sun," said Scarface; "I am trying to find where he lives, so that I may ask him for her."

"Ah," said the wolverene, "I know where he lives. It is nearly night now, but to-morrow I will show you the trail to the big water. He lives on the other side of it."

Early in the morning they set out, and the wolverene showed Scarface the trail, and he followed it until he came to the water's edge.

When he looked out over it, his heart almost stopped. Never before had any one seen such a great water. The other side could not be seen and there was no end to it. Scarface sat down on the shore. This seemed the end. His food was gone; his moccasins were worn out; he had no longer strength, no longer courage; his heart was sick. "I cannot cross this great water," he said. "I cannot return to the people. Here by this water I shall die."

Yet, even as he thought this, helpers were near. Two swans came swimming up to the shore and said to him, "Why have you come here? What are you doing? It is very far to the place where your people live."

"I have come here to die," replied Scarface. "Far away in my country is a beautiful girl. I want to marry her, but she belongs to the Sun; so I set out to find him and ask him for her. I have travelled many days. My food is gone. I cannot go back; I cannot cross this great water; so I must die."

"No," said the swans; "it shall not be so. Across this water is the home of that Above

97

Person.   Get on our backs, and we will take you
there."

Scarface stood up.   Now he felt strong and
full of courage.   He waded out into the water
and lay down on the swans' backs, and they
swam away.   It was a fearful journey, for that
water was deep and black, and in it live strange
people and great animals which might reach up
and seize a person and pull him down under the
water; yet the swans carried Scarface safely
to the other side.   There was seen a broad, hard
trail leading back from the water's edge.

"There," said the swans; "you are now close
to the Sun's lodge.   Follow that trail, and soon
you will see it."

Scarface started to walk along the trail, and
after he had gone a little way he came to some
beautiful things lying in the trail.   There was
a war shirt, a shield, a bow, and a quiver of
arrows.   He had never seen such fine weapons.
He looked at them, but he did not touch them,
and at last walked around them and went on.
A little farther along he met a young man, a
very handsome person.   His hair was long; his

clothing was made of strange skins, and his moccasins were sewed with bright feathers.

The young man spoke to him and asked, "Did you see some weapons lying in the trail?"

"Yes," replied Scarface, "I saw them."

"Did you touch them?" said the young man.

"No," said Scarface; "I supposed some one had left them there, and I did not touch them."

"You do not meddle with the property of others," said the young man. "What is your name, and where are you going?" Scarface told him. Then said the young man, "My name is Early Riser (the morning star). The Sun is my father. Come, I will take you to our lodge. My father is not at home now, but he will return at night."

At length they came to the lodge. It was large and handsome, and on it were painted strange medicine animals. On a tripod behind the lodge were the Sun's weapons and his war clothing. Scarface was ashamed to go into the lodge, but Morning Star said, "Friend, do not be afraid; we are glad you have come."

When they went in a woman was sitting

99

there, the Moon, the Sun's wife and the mother of Morning Star. She spoke to Scarface kindly and gave him food to eat, and when he had eaten she asked, "Why have you come so far from your people?"

So Scarface told her about the beautiful girl that he wished to marry and said, "She belongs to the Sun. I have come to ask him for her."

When it was almost night, and time for the Sun to come home, the Moon hid Scarface under a pile of robes. As soon as the Sun got to the doorway he said, "A strange person is here."

"Yes, father," said Morning Star, "a young man has come to see you. He is a good young man, for he found some of my things in the trail and did not touch them."

Scarface came out from under the robes and the Sun entered the lodge and sat down. He spoke to Scarface and said, "I am glad you have come to our lodge. Stay with us as long as you like. Sometimes my son is lonely. Be his friend."

The next day the two young men were talking about going hunting and the Moon spoke to Scarface and said, "Go with my son where you like, but do not hunt near that big water. Do not let him go there. That is the home of great birds with long, sharp bills. They kill people. I have had many sons, but these birds have killed them all. Only Morning Star is left."

Scarface stayed a long time in the Sun's lodge, and every day went hunting with Morning Star. One day they came near the water and saw the big birds.

"Come on," said Morning Star, "let us go and kill those birds."

"No, no," said Scarface, "we must not go there. Those are terrible birds; they will kill us."

Morning Star would not listen. He ran toward the water and Scarface ran after him, for he knew that he must kill the birds and save the boy's life. He ran ahead of Morning Star and met the birds, which were coming to fight, and killed every one of them with his spear; not one was left. The young men cut off the heads of the birds and carried them home, and when Morning Star's mother heard what they had done, and they showed her the birds' heads, she was glad. She cried over the two young men and called Scarface "My son," and when the Sun came home at night she told him about it, and he too was glad.

"My son," he said to Scarface, "I will not forget what you have this day done for me. Tell me now what I can do for you; what is your trouble?"

"Alas, alas!" replied Scarface, "Pity me. I came here to ask you for that girl. I want to marry her. I asked her and she was glad, but she says that she belongs to you, and that you told her not to marry."

"What you say is true," replied the Sun. "I have seen the days and all that she has done. Now I give her to you. She is yours. I am glad that she has been wise, and I know that she has never done wrong. The Sun takes care of good women; they shall live a long time, and so shall their husbands and children.

"Now, soon you will go home. I wish to tell you something and you must be wise and listen. I am the only chief; everything is mine; I

102

made the earth, the mountains, the prairies, the rivers, and the forests; I made the people and all the animals. This is why I say that I alone am chief. I can never die. It is true the winter makes me old and weak, but every summer I grow young again.

"What one of all the animals is the smartest?" the Sun went on. "It is the raven, for he always finds food; he is never hungry. Which one of all the animals is the most to be reverenced? It is the buffalo; of all the animals I like him best. He is for the people; he is your food and your shelter. What part of his body is sacred? It is the tongue; that belongs to me. What else is sacred? Berries. They too are mine. Come with me now and see the world."

The Sun took Scarface to the edge of the sky and they looked down and saw the world. It is flat and round, and all around the edge it goes straight down. Then said the Sun, "If any man is sick or in danger his wife may promise to build me a lodge if he recovers. If the woman is good, then I shall be pleased and help the man; but if she is not good, or if she lies, then I shall be angry. You shall build the lodge like the world, round, with walls, but first you must build a sweat-lodge of one hundred sticks. It shall be arched like the sky, and one-half of it shall be painted red for me, the other half you shall paint black for the night." He told Scarface all about making the Medicine Lodge, and when he had finished speaking, he rubbed some medicine on the young man's face and the scar that had been there disappeared. He gave him two raven feathers, saying: "These are a sign for the girl that I give her to you. They must always be worn by the husband of the woman who builds a Medicine Lodge."

Now Scarface was ready to return home. The Sun and Morning Star gave him many good presents; the Moon cried and kissed him and was sorry to see him go. Then the Sun showed him the short trail. It was the Wolf Road— the Milky Way. He followed it and soon reached the ground.

It was a very hot day. All the lodge skins were raised and the people sat in the shade.

104

There was a chief, a very generous man, who all day long was calling out for feasts, and people kept coming to his lodge to eat and smoke with him. Early in the morning this chief saw sitting on a butte near by a person close-wrapped in his robe. All day long this person sat there and did not move. When it was almost night the chief said, "That person has sat there all day in the strong heat, and he has not eaten nor drunk. Perhaps he is a stranger. Go and ask him to come to my lodge."

Some young men ran up to the person and said to him, "Why have you sat here all day in the great heat? Come to the shade of the lodges. The chief asks you to eat with him." The person rose and threw off his robe and the young men were surprised. He wore fine clothing; his bow, shield, and other weapons were of strange make; but they knew his face, although the scar was gone, and they ran ahead, shouting, "The Scarface poor young man has come. He is poor no longer. The scar on his face is gone."

All the people hurried out to see him and to

ask him questions. "Where did you get all these fine things?" He did not answer. There in the crowd stood that young woman, and, taking the two raven feathers from his head, he gave them to her and said, "The trail was long and I nearly died, but by those helpers I found his lodge. He is glad. He sends these feathers to you. They are the sign."

Great was her gladness then. They were married and made the first Medicine Lodge, as the Sun had said. The Sun was glad. He gave them great age. They were never sick. When they were very old, one morning their children called to them, "Awake, rise and eat." They did not move.

In the night, together, in sleep, without pain, their shadows had departed to the Sandhills.

THE BUFFALO–PAINTED LODGES

THE old lodges of the Piegans were made of buffalo skin and were painted with pictures of different kinds—birds, or animals, or trees, or mountains. It is believed that in most cases the first painter of any lodge was taught how he should paint it in a dream, but this was not always the case.

Two of the most important lodges in the Blackfeet camp are known as the Inĭs′kĭm lodges. Both are painted with figures of buffalo, one with black buffalo, and the other with yellow buffalo. Certain of the Inĭs′kĭm are kept in these lodges and can be kept in no others.

This story tells how these two lodges came to be made.

The painters were told what to do long, long ago, "in about the second generation after the first people."

In those days the old Piegans lived in the

north, close to the Red Deer River. The camp moved, and the lodges were pitched on the river. One day two old men who were close friends had gone out from the camp to find some straight cherry shoots with which to make arrows. After they had gathered their shafts, they sat down on a high bank by the river and began to peel the bark from the shoots. The river was high. One of these men was named Weasel Heart and the other Fisher.

As they sat there, Weasel Heart chanced to look down into the water and saw something. He said to his comrade, "Friend, do you not see something down there where the water goes around?"

Fisher said, "No; I see nothing except buffalo," for he was looking across the river to the other side, and not down into the water.

"No," said Weasel Heart; "I do not mean over there on the prairie. Look down into that deep hole in the river, and you will see a lodge there."

Fisher looked as he had been told, and saw the lodge.

Weasel Heart said, "There is a lodge painted

with black buffalo." As he spoke thus, Fisher said, "I see another lodge, standing in front of it." Weasel Heart saw that lodge too—the yellow-painted-buffalo lodge.

The two men wondered at this and could not understand how it could be, but they were both men of strong hearts, and presently Weasel Heart said, "Friend, I shall go down to enter that lodge. Do you sit here and tell me when I get to the place." Then Weasel Heart went up the river and found a drift-log to support him and pushed it out into the water, and floated down toward the cut bank. When he had reached the place where the lodge stood Fisher told him, and he let go the log and dived down into the water and entered the lodge.

In it he found two persons who owned the lodge, a man and his wife. The man said to him, "You are welcome," and Weasel Heart sat down. Then spoke the owner of the lodge saying, "My son, this is my lodge, and I give it to you. Look well at it inside and outside; and make your lodge like this. If you do that it may be a help to you."

Fisher sat a long time waiting for his friend, but at last he looked down the stream and saw a man on the shore walking toward him. He came along the bank until he had reached his friend. It was Weasel Heart.

Fisher said to him, "I have been waiting a long time, and I was afraid that something bad had happened to you."

Weasel Heart asked him, "Did you see me?"

"I saw you," said Fisher, "when you went into that lodge. Did you, when you came out of the lodge, see there in the water another lodge painted with yellow buffalo? Is it still there?"

Weasel Heart said, "I saw it; it is there. Go you into the water as I did."

Then Fisher went up the stream as his friend had gone and entered the water at the same place and swam down as Weasel Heart had done, and when Weasel Heart showed him the place he dived down and disappeared as Weasel Heart had disappeared. He entered the yellow-painted-buffalo lodge, and his friend saw him go into it.

In the lodge were two persons, a man and his

wife. The man said to him, "You are welcome; sit there." He spoke further, saying, "My son, you have seen this lodge of mine; I give it to you. Look carefully at it, inside and outside, and fix up your lodge in that way. It may be a help to you hereafter." Then Fisher went out.

Weasel Heart waited for his friend as long as Fisher had waited for him, and when Fisher came out of the water it was at the place where Weasel Heart had come out. Then the two friends went home to the camp.

When the two had come to a hill near the camp they met a young man, and by him sent word that the people should make a sweat-house for them. After the sweat-house had been made, word was sent to them, and they entered the camp and went into the sweat-house and took a sweat, and all the time while they were sweating, sand was falling from their bodies.

Some time after that the people moved camp and went out and killed buffalo, and these two men made two lodges, and painted them just as the lodges were painted that they had seen in the river.

These two men had strong power which came to them from the Under-water People.

Once the people wished to cross the river, but the stream was deep and it was always hard for them to get across. Often the dogs and the travois were swept away and the people lost many of their things. At this time the tribe wished to cross, and Fisher and Weasel Heart said to each other, "The people want to cross the river, but it is high and they cannot do so. Let us try to make a crossing, so that it will be easier for them." So Weasel Heart alone crossed the river and sat on the bank on the other side, and Fisher sat opposite to him on the bank where the camp was.

Then Fisher said to the people, "Pack up your things now and get ready to cross. I will make a place where you can cross easily."

Weasel Heart and Fisher filled their pipes and smoked, and then each started to cross the river. As each stepped into the water, the river began to go down and the crossing grew more and more shallow. The people with all their dogs followed close behind Fisher, as he had told them to do. Fisher and Weasel Heart met in the middle of the river, and when they met they stepped to one side up the stream and let the people pass them. Ever since that day this has been a shallow crossing.

These lodges came from the Under-water People—Sū′yē-tŭp′pĭ. They were those who had owned them and who had been kind to Weasel Heart and Fisher.

MĪKA'PI—RED OLD MAN

IN Montana, running into the Missouri River from the south, is a little stream that the Blackfeet call "It Fell on Them." Once, long, long ago, while a number of women were digging in a bank near this stream for the red earth that they used as paint, the bank gave way and fell on them, burying and killing them. The white people call this Armell's Creek.

It was on this stream near the mountains that the Piegans were camped when Mīka'pi went to war. This was long ago.

Early in the morning a herd of buffalo had been seen feeding on the slopes of the mountains, and some hunters went out to kill them. Travelling carefully up the ravines, and keeping out of sight of the herd, they came close to them, near enough to shoot their arrows, and they began to kill fat cows. But while they were doing this a war party of Snakes that had been

114

hidden on the mountainside attacked them, and the Piegans began to run back toward their camp.

One of them, called Fox Eye, was a brave man, and shouted to the others to stop and wait, saying, "Let us fight these people; the Snakes are not brave; we can drive them back." But the other Piegans would not listen to him; they made excuses, saying, "We have no shields; our war medicine is not here; there are many of them; why should we stop here to die?" They ran on to the camp, but Fox Eye would not run. Hiding behind a rock he prepared to fight, but as he was looking for some enemy to shoot at, holding his arrow on the string, a Snake had crept up on the bank above him; the Piegan heard the twang of the bowstring, and the long, fine arrow passed through his body. His bow and arrow dropped from his hands, and he fell forward, dead. Now, too late, the warriors came rushing out from the Piegan camp to help him, but the Snakes scalped their enemy, scattered up the mountain, and soon were hidden in the timber.

Fox Eye had two wives, and their father and mother and all their near relations were dead. All Fox Eye's relations had died. So it happened that these poor widows had no one to help them—no one to take vengeance for the killing of their husband.

All day long, and often far into the night, these two sat on a near-by hill and wailed, and their mourning was sad.

There was a young man named Mīka'pi. Every morning when he awoke he heard the mourning of these poor widows, and all through the day he could not forget their sorrow. He pitied them. One day he sent his mother to them, to tell them that he wished to speak with them. When they had come to the lodge they entered and sat down close by the doorway and covered their heads.

"Listen!" said Mīka'pi. "For days and nights I have heard your mourning, and I too have mourned. Your husband was my close friend, and now he is dead, and no relations are left to avenge him. So now I say to you, I will take the load from your hearts; I will go to war and kill enemies and take scalps, and when I return they shall be yours. I will wipe away your tears, and we shall be glad that Fox Eye is avenged."

When the people heard that Mĭka'pi was going to war many young men wished to join him, but he refused. "I shall go alone," he said. So when he had taken a medicine sweat and had asked a priest to pray for him in his absence, he left the camp one evening, just as it was growing dark.

It is only the foolish warrior who travels in the day. The wise one knows that war-parties may be out, or that some camp watcher sitting on a hill may see him far off and may try to kill him. Mĭka'pi was not one of these foolish persons. He was brave and cautious, and he had powerful helpers. Some have said that he was helped by the ghosts. When he started to war against the Snakes he travelled in low places, and at sunrise he climbed some hill near by and looked carefully over the country in all directions, and during all the long day he lay there and watched, sleeping often, but only for a short time.

117

When Mīka'pi had come to the Great Place of Falling Water,* it began to rain hard, and, looking about for a place to sleep, he saw a hole in the rocks and crept in and lay down at the farther end. The rain did not stop, and when it grew dark he could not travel because of the darkness and the storm, so he lay down to sleep again; but before he had fallen asleep he heard something at the mouth of the cave, and then something creeping toward him. Then soon something touched his breast, and he put out his hand and felt a person. Then he sat up.

Mīka'pi stretched out his hand and put its palm on the person's breast and moved his hand quickly from side to side, and then touched the person with the point of his finger, which in sign language means, "Who are you?" The stranger took Mīka'pi's hand and made him feel of his own right hand. The thumb and fingers were closed except the forefinger, which was extended. When Mīka'pi's hand was on the stranger's hand the person moved his hand forward with a zigzag motion, meaning Snake.

* The Great Falls of the Missouri.

118

Mīka'pi was glad. Here had come to him one of the tribe he was seeking, yet he thought it better to wait for a time before fighting him; so when, in signs, the Snake asked Mīka'pi who he was he replied, by making the sign for paddling a canoe, that he was a River person, for he knew that the Snakes and the River people, or Pend d'Oreilles, were at peace. Then the two lay down for the night, but Mīka'pi did not sleep. Through the long night he watched for the first light, so that he might kill his enemy; and just at daybreak Mīka'pi, without noise, strung his bow, fitted an arrow to the string, and sent the thin shaft through his enemy's heart. The Snake half rose up and fell back dead. Mīka'pi scalped him, took his bow and arrows and his bundle of moccasins, and went out of the cave and looked all about. Daylight had come, but no one was in sight. Perhaps, like himself, the Snake had gone to war alone. Mīka'pi did not forget to be careful because he had been fortunate. He travelled only a little way, and then hid himself and waited for night before going on. After drinking from the river he ate and, climbing up on a high rock wall, he slept.

He dreamed that he fought with strange people and was wounded. He felt blood trickling from his wounds, and when he awoke he knew that he had been warned to turn back. Other signs were bad. He saw an eagle rising carrying a snake, which dropped from its claws. The setting sun too was painted, a sure warning that danger was near. In spite of all these things Mīka'pi determined to go on. He thought of the poor widows mourning; he thought of the welcome of the people if he should return with scalps; he thought also of two young sisters whom he wished to marry. If he could return with proof of brave deeds, they would think well of him.

Mīka'pi travelled onward.

The sun had already disappeared behind the sharp pointed dark peaks of the mountains. It was nearly night. As the light grew dim, the far stretching prairie began to be hidden. By a stream in a valley where grew large and small trees were the lodges of a great camp. For a long distance up and down the river rose the smokes of many fires.

On a hill overlooking the valley sat a person alone. His robe was drawn close about him, and he sat there without moving, looking down on the valley and out on the prairie above it. Perhaps he was watching for enemies; perhaps he was praying.

Creeping through the grass behind this person, something was slowly drawing near to him. There was no noise, the watcher heard nothing; still he sat there, looking out over the prairie, and turning his head neither to the right nor the left. This thing behind him kept creeping closer, and presently it was so near it could touch the man. Perhaps then there was some little rustle of the grass, and the watcher turned his head. It was too late. A strong arm around his neck bent his head back, a hand covered his mouth, a long stone knife was thrust into his breast, and he died in silence. The fading light had kept people in the camp from seeing what had happened.

The man who had used the knife scalped his enemy, and slowly, hidden by the grass, crept down the hill that he had just ascended, and when he reached the cover of a low place Mīka'pi rose to his feet and crept away. He had another Snake scalp tied to his belt. His heart was glad, but he was not satisfied.

Several nights had passed since the signs warned him to turn back, but notwithstanding the warnings, he had succeeded. Perhaps his success had made him too confident. He longed for more of it. "One more scalp I shall take," he said, "and then I will return to the people."

He climbed far up the mountainside and hid among the pines and slept, but when day came he awoke and crept out to a point where he could see the camp. He saw the smoke rising as the women kindled their morning fires; he saw the people going about through the camp, and then presently he saw many people rush up on the hill where he had left the dead enemy. He could not hear their angry cries, nor their mournful wailings, but he knew how badly they felt, and he sung a song, for he was happy.

Once more the sun had disappeared behind the mountains, and as darkness grew Mīka'pi came down from where he had been hiding and carefully approached the camp. Now was a time of danger. Now watchers might be hidden anywhere, looking for the approach of enemies, ready to raise a cry to warn the camp. Each bush or clump of rye grass or willow thicket might hide an enemy. Very slowly, looking and listening, Mīka'pi crept around the outskirts of the camp. He made no noise, he did not show himself. Presently he heard some one clear his throat and then a cough, and a little bush moved. Here was a watcher. Could he kill him and get away? He sat and waited to see what would happen, for he knew where his enemy was, but the enemy knew nothing of him. The great moon rose over the eastern prairie and climbed high and began to travel across the sky. Seven Persons swung around and pointed downward. It was about the middle of the night. At length the person in the bush grew tired of watching; he thought no enemy could be near and he rose and stretched out his arms and yawned, but even as he stood an arrow pierced him through, beneath the arms. He gave a loud cry and tried to run, but another arrow struck him, and he fell.

And now from out the camp rushed the warriors toward the sound, but even as they came Mĭka′pi had taken the scalp from his enemy and started to run away into the darkness. The moon was bright, and close behind him were the Snakes. He heard arrows flying by him, and presently one passed through his arm. He pulled it out and threw it from him. Another struck his leg, and he fell, and a great shout arose from thé Snakes. Now their enemy was down and revenge for the two lives lately taken was certain.

But Mĭka′pi's helpers were not far off. It was at the very verge of a high cut wall overhanging the river that Mĭka′pi fell, and even as the Snakes shouted he rolled over the brink into the dark rushing water below. The Snakes ran along the edge of the river, looking into the water, with bent bows watching for the enemy's head or body to appear, but they saw nothing.

Carefully they looked along the shores and sandbars; they did not find him.

Mīka'pi had sunk deep in the water. The swift current carried him along, and when he rose to the surface he was beyond his enemies. For some time he floated on, but the arrow in his leg pained him and at last he crept out on a sandbar. He managed to draw the arrow from his leg, and finding at the edge of the bar a dry log, he rolled it into the water, and keeping his hands on it, drifted down the river with the current. Cold and stiff from his wounds, he crept out on the bank and lay down in the warm sunshine. Soon he fell asleep.

When he awoke the sun was in the middle of the sky. His leg and arm were swollen and pained him, yet he started to go home, and for a time struggled onward; but at last, tired and discouraged, he sat down.

"Ah," he said to himself, "true were the signs! How crazy I was to go against them! Now my bravery has been useless, for here I must stop and die. The widows will still mourn, and who will care for my father and

125

mother in their old age? Pity me now, O Sun; help me, O Great Above Person! Give me life!"

Something was coming through the brush near him, breaking the sticks as it walked. Was it the Snakes following his trail? Mīka'pi strung his bow and drew his arrows from the quiver. He waited.

No, it was not a Snake; it was a bear, a big grizzly bear, standing there looking down at Mīka'pi. "What is my brother doing here?" said the bear. "Why does he pray for life?"

"Look at my leg," said Mīka'pi; "swollen and sore. See my wounded arm; I can hardly hold the bow. Far away is the home of my people, and my strength is gone. Surely here I must die, for I cannot walk, and I have no food."

"Take courage, my brother," said the bear. "Keep up a strong heart, for I will help you, and you shall have life."

When he had said this he lifted Mīka'pi in his arms and took him to a place where there was thick mud, and there he took great handfuls of the mud and plastered it on the wounds, and while he was putting on the mud he sang a medicine song. Then he carried Mīka'pi to a place where there were many service berries, and he broke off great branches of the fruit and gave them to him, saying, "Eat, my brother, eat." He kept breaking off branches full of large, ripe berries until Mīka'pi was full and could eat no more.

Then said the bear, "Now lie down on my back and hold tight by my hair and we will go on"; and when Mīka'pi had got on his back and was ready the bear started. All through the night he travelled on without stopping, and when morning came they rested for a time and ate more berries, and again the bear put mud upon the man's wounds. In this way they travelled on, until, on the fourth day, they had come close to the lodges of the Piegans and the people saw them coming, and wondered.

"Get off now, my brother, get off," said the bear. "There is the camp of your people. I shall leave you"; and at once he turned and went off up the mountain.

All the people came out to meet Mīka'pi, and they carried him to his father's lodge. He untied the scalps from his belt and gave them to the poor widows, saying, "These are the scalps of your enemies; I wipe away your tears." Then every one rejoiced. All Mīka'pi's women relations went through the camp, shouting out his name and singing songs about him, and all prepared to dance the dance of triumph and rejoicing.

First came the widows. They carried the scalps tied on poles, and their faces were painted black. Then came the medicine men, with their medicine pipes unwrapped, and then the bands of the All Friends dressed in their war costumes; then came the old men; and, last of all, the women and children. They went all through the village, stopping here and there to dance, and Mīka'pi sat outside the lodge and saw all the people dance by him. He forgot his pain and was happy, and although he could not dance, he sung with them.

Soon they made the medicine lodge, and first of all the warriors, Mīka'pi was chosen to cut the rawhide to bind the poles, and as he cut the strips he related the coups he had counted. He told of the enemies he had killed, and all the people shouted his name and the drummers struck the drum. The father of those two sisters gave them to him. He was glad to have such a son-in-law.

Long lived Mīka'pi. Of all the great chiefs who have lived and died he was the greatest. He did many other great things. It must be true, as the old men have said, that he was helped by the ghosts, for no one can do such things without help from those fearful and terrible persons.

RED ROBE'S DREAM

LONG, long ago, Red Robe and Talking Rock were young men in the Blackfeet camp. In their childhood days and early youth their life had been hard. Talking Rock was an orphan without a single relation and Red Robe had only his old grandmother.

This old woman, by hard work and sacrifice, had managed to rear the boys. She tanned robes for the hunters, made them moccasins worked with porcupine quills, and did everything she could to get a little food or worn out robes and hide, from which she made clothes for her boys. They never had new, brightly painted calf robes, like other children. They went barefoot in summer, and in winter their toes often showed through the worn out skin of their moccasins. They had no flesh. Their ribs could be counted beneath the skin; their cheeks were hollow; they looked always hungry.

When they grew to be twelve or fifteen years old they began to do better, for now they could do more and more for themselves. They herded horses and performed small services for the wealthy men; then, too, they hunted and killed a little meat. Now, for their work, three or four dogs were given them, so with the two the old woman owned, they were able to pack their small lodge and other possessions when the camp moved, instead of carrying everything on their backs.

Now they began to do their best to make life easier for the good old woman who had worked so hard to keep them from starving and freezing.

Time passed. The boys grew old enough to go out and fast. They had their dreams. Each found his secret helper of mysterious power, and each became a warrior. Still they were very poor, compared with other young men of their age. They had bows, but only a few arrows. They were not able to pay some great medicine man to make shields for them. As yet they went to war only as servants.

About this time Red Robe fell in love.

In the camp was a beautiful girl named
Mā-mĭn'—the Wing—whom all the young men
wished to marry, but perhaps Red Robe loved
her more than all the rest. Her father was a
rich old medicine man who never invited any
except chiefs and great warriors to feast with
him, and Red Robe seldom entered his lodge.
He used to dress as well as he could, to braid
his hair carefully, to paint his face nicely, and to
stand for a long time near the lodge looking
entreatingly at her as she came and went about
her work, or fleshed a robe under the shelter
of some travois over which a hide was spread.
Then whenever they met, he thought the look
she gave him in passing was friendly—perhaps
more than that.

Wherever Mā-mĭn' went her mother or some
woman of the family went with her, so Red
Robe could never speak to her, but he was
often near by. One day, when she was gathering wood for the lodge, and her companion was
out of sight behind some willow bushes some
distance away, Red Robe had a chance to tell
Mā-mĭn' what was in his heart. He walked

up to her and took her hands in his, and she did not try to draw them away. He said to her, "I love you; I cannot remember a time when I saw you that my heart did not beat faster. I am poor, very poor, and it is useless to ask your father to let me marry you, for he will not consent; but there is another way, and if you love me, you will do what I ask. Let us go from here—far away. We will find some tribe that will be kind to us, and even if we fail in that we can live in some way. Now, if you love me, and I hope you do, you will come."

"Ai," replied Mā-mĭn', "I do love you; only you. All the other young men pass before me as shadows. I scarcely see them, but I cannot do what you ask. I cannot go away and leave my mother to mourn; she who loves me so well. Let us wait a little. Go to war. Do something great and brave. Then perhaps you will not uselessly ask my father to give me to you."

In vain Red Robe tried to persuade the girl to do as he wished. She was kind; she threw her arms about him and kissed him and cried, but she would not run away to leave her mother to sorrow, to be beaten by her father, who would blame the poor woman for all the disgrace; and so, too soon, they parted, for they heard her companion coming—the sound of her heavy footsteps.

Three Bulls, chief of the camp, was a great man. He had a fierce temper, and when he spoke, people hurried to do what he ordered, for they feared him. He never talked loud nor called any one by an ill name. When any one displeased him or refused to do what he said he just smiled and then killed the person. He was brave. In battle with enemies he was the equal of twenty men, rushing here, there, into the thickest of the fights, and killing—always with that silent, terrible smile on his face. Because he was such a great warrior, and also because he was generous, helping the poor, feasting any who came to his lodge, he was the head chief of the Blackfeet.

Three Bulls had several wives and many children, some of them grown and married. Gray hairs were now many in his head. His face wrinkles showed that old age was not far distant.

No one supposed that he would ever take another wife; so when the news spread through the camp that he had asked the old medicine man for his daughter Mā-mĭn', every one was surprised. When Red Robe heard the news his heart nearly broke. The old medicine man agreed to let the chief have the girl. He dared not refuse, nor did he wish to, for many good presents were to be given him in three days' time. When that was done, he told his daughter, she would be taken to the chief's lodge; let her prepare for the change.

That day Red Robe had planned to start with a party to war; but when he heard this news he asked his friend Talking Rock to take word to the leader that he had changed his mind and would not go. He asked his friend to stay with him, instead of joining the war party, and Talking Rock agreed to do so.

Out in front of the camp was a large spring, and to that place Red Robe went and stood leaning against a large stone and looking sadly down into the blue water. Soon, as he had thought, Mā-mĭn' came to the spring for a skin of water.

He took her hands, as he had done before, and began to beg her to go away with him that very night, before it was too late. The girl cried bitterly, but at first she did not speak.

The two were standing in plain sight of the camp and the people in it, and some one went to the chief's lodge and told him what was taking place.

"Go to the spring," said the chief, "and tell that young man to let the girl go; she is to be my wife."

The person did as he was told, but the two young people paid no attention to him. They did not care what any one said, nor if the whole camp saw them there together. All they could think about was this terrible thing, which would make them unhappy so long as they lived. Red Robe kept asking the girl to go, and at last she consented to do as he wished. They had their arms about each other, not thinking of the crowd that was watching them, and were quickly planning for their meeting and for their going away that night, when Three Bulls quietly walked up to them and stabbed the young man with a flint-pointed lance. Red Robe sank down dying at the young girl's feet, and she, looking down for an instant at her lover, turned and ran to her father's lodge.

"Bring wood," the chief called out; "let every one bring some wood; all you have at your lodges. Those who have none, let them go quickly and bring some from the timber."

All the people hurried to obey. What Three Bulls ordered was soon done, for the people feared him, and soon a great pile of wood was heaped beside the dead man.

The chief lifted the slender young form, placed it on the pile of wood, and told a woman to bring coals and set fire to the pile. When this had been done, all left the place except Three Bulls, who stayed there, tending the fire and poking it here and there, until it was burnt out and no wood or trace of a human body was left. Nothing remained except the little pile of ashes. These he scattered. Still he was not satisfied. His medicine was strong; perhaps his dream had warned him. Now he ordered that the lodges be taken down, that everything be packed up, and that the trail of the moving camp should pass over the heap of ashes.

Some time before this, after Red Robe had made his long fasting, and his dream had come to him and he had returned to his grandmother's lodge, he had told his true friend something of what had been said to him by his dream.

"If I should die," he said, "and you are near, do not desert me. Go to the place where I fell, and if my body should have been destroyed look carefully around the place. If you can find even a shred of my flesh or a bit of my bone, it will be well. So said my dream. Here are four arrows, which the dream told me to make. If you can find a bit of my body, flesh or bone, or even hair, cover it with a robe, and standing over it, shoot three arrows one after another up into the air, crying, as each one leaves the bow, 'Look out!' When you fit the fourth arrow on the bowstring and shoot it upward, cry, 'Look out, Red Robe, the arrow will strike you!' and as you say this, turn and run away from the place, not looking back as you go. If you do this, my friend, just as I have told you, I shall live again."

As the camp moved, Three Bulls stood and watched it filing over the place of the fire, and saw the ashes scattered by the trailing ends of lodge poles and travois, and by the feet of hundreds of people and dogs. Still he was not satisfied, and for a long time after the last of the people had passed he remained there. Then he went on across the flat and up and over a ridge, but presently he returned, once, twice, four times, to the crest of the hill and looked back at the place where the camp had been; but at last he felt sure that no one remained at the place, and went on.

Yet Talking Rock was there. He had been hidden in the brush all the time, watching the chief. Even after Three Bulls had passed over the ridge, he remained crouched in the bushes, and saw him come back again and again to peer over its crest. Still further on there was another higher ridge, and when the young man saw Three Bulls climb that and disappear on the trail of the camp, he came forth.

Going to the place where his friend had lain, Talking Rock sat down and mourned, wailing long and loud. Back on the hills the wolves and coyotes heard him and they too became sorrowful, adding their cries to his.

The young man had little faith in the power of the four arrows that he kept so carefully wrapped in a separate bundle in his quiver. He looked at the place where Red Robe's body had been burnt. It was like any other place on the great trail that had been made, dust and grass blades mingled together, and scratches made by the dragging poles. It did not seem possible that anything of his friend's body remained; yet he must search, and breaking a green willow twig he began carefully to work over the dust, stopping his crying, for the tears blinded his eyes so that he could not see.

All the long morning and far into the afternoon, Talking Rock swept the dust this way and that, turning it over and over, in a circle that grew always wider, and just as he was about to give up the search, he found a bit of charred and blackened bone. Was this a part of his friend's frame? Was it not more likely a bit of bone of buffalo or elk, which some dog had carried from one of the fireplaces of the camp and dropped here?

Now for the test. Talking Rock covered the bit of bone with his robe as he had been told to do. He even raised the robe along its middle, making it look as if it really covered a person lying there. Then he shot three of the arrows up in the air, each time crying, "Look out."

Then with a hand that trembled a little, he drew the fourth arrow from the quiver, shot it and cried, "Look out, Red Robe, the arrow will strike you"; and, turning, ran from the place with all his speed.

How he wanted to look back! How he longed to see if his friend was really rising from that bit of blackened bone! But Talking Rock was strong-hearted. He controlled his desires. On and on he ran, and then—behind him the light tread of running feet, a firm hand gripped his shoulder, and a loved voice said, "Why so fast, my friend?" and stopping and turning, Talking Rock found himself face to face with Red Robe.

He could not believe what he saw, and had to pinch himself and to hold his friend hard in his arms to believe that all this was real.

The camp had not moved far, and the lodges were pitched on the next stream to the south. Soon after dark, the two friends entered it and went to their lodge. The poor old grandmother could not believe her eyes when she saw the young man she had reared and loved so dearly; but when he spoke she knew that it was he, and running over to him she held him in her arms and kissed him, crying from joy. After a little time, the young man said to her, "Grandmother, go to the chief's lodge and say to him that I, Red Robe, need some dried meat." The old woman hesitated at this strange request, but Red Robe said: "Go, do not fear him; Three Bulls is now the one to know fear."

When the old woman entered the great lodge and in reply to the chief's look said, "Red Robe sent me here. He wants some dried meat," only Three Bulls of all who were in the lodge, showed no surprise. "It is what I expected," he said; "in spite of all my care he lives again, and

142

I can do nothing." Turning to his wives he said, "Give her meat."

"Did you see Mā-mĭn'?" asked Red Robe, when his grandmother had returned with the meat and had told him what the chief had said.

"No, she was not in the lodge, but two women were approaching as I left it. I think they were the girl and her mother."

"Go back once more," said the young man, "and tell Three Bulls to send me that young woman."

But now the poor old grandmother was afraid. "I dare not tell him that," she exclaimed. "He would kill me, and you. His anger would be fearful."

"Do not fear," said Red Robe, "do not fear, my mother, his anger and his power are no longer to be feared. He is as feeble and as helpless as one of those old bulls one sees on the sunny side of the coulée, spending his last days before the wolves pull him down."

The old woman went to the lodge and told the chief what Red Robe further wished. Mā-mĭn' was there, her head covered with her robe, crying quietly, and Three Bulls told her to arise and go with the messenger. Timidly at first, and then with steps that broke into a run, Mā-mĭn' hurried toward the lodge of her sweetheart and entered it. With a cry of joy she threw herself into his arms, and Talking Rock went out and left them alone.

Great now was the happiness of these young people. Long was their life, full of plenty and of great honor. Red Robe became a chief, respected and loved by all the people. Mā-mĭn' bore him many children, who grew up to be the support of their old age.

THE BLACKFEET CREATION

THE Blackfeet believe that the Sun made the earth—that he is the creator. One of the names by which they call the Sun is Napi —Old Man. This is how they tell of the creation:

In the beginning there was water everywhere; nothing else was to be seen. There was something floating on the water, and on this raft were Old Man and all the animals.

Old Man wished to make land, and he told the beaver to dive down to the bottom of the water and to try to bring up a little mud. The beaver dived and was under water for a long time, but he could not reach the bottom. Then the loon tried, and after him the otter, but the water was too deep for them. At last the musk-rat was sent down, and he was gone for a long time; so long that they thought he must be drowned, but at last he came up and floated almost dead on the water, and when they pulled him up on the raft and looked at his paws, they found a little mud in them. When Old Man had dried this mud, he scattered it over the water and land was formed. This is the story told by the Blackfeet. It is very much like one told by some Eastern Indians, who are related to the Blackfeet.

After the land had been made, Old Man travelled about on it, making things and fixing up the earth so as to suit him. First, he marked out places where he wished the rivers to run, sometimes making them run smoothly, and again, in some places, putting falls on them. He made the mountains and the prairie, the timber and the small trees and bushes, and sometimes he carried along with him a lot of rocks, from which he built some of the mountains—as the Sweet Grass Hills—which stand out on the prairie by themselves.

Old Man caused grass to grow on the plains, so that the animals might have something to feed on. He marked off certain pieces of land, where he caused different kinds of roots and berries to grow—a place for camas; and one for wild carrots; one for wild turnips, sweet root and bitter root; one for service berries, bullberries, cherries, plums, and rosebuds.

He made all kinds of animals that travel on the ground. When he made the big-horn with its great horns, he put it out on the prairie. It did not seem to travel easily there; it was awkward and could not go fast, so he took it by one of its horns and led it up into the rough hills and among the rocks, and let it go there, and it skipped about among the cliffs and easily went up fearful places. So Old Man said to the big-horn, "This is the place for you; this is what you are fitted for; the rough country and the mountains." While he was in the mountains he made the antelope, and turned it loose to see how it travelled. The antelope ran so fast that it fell over some rocks and hurt itself. He saw that this would not do, and took the antelope down on the prairie and set it free there, and it ran away fast and gracefully, and he said to it, "This is the place that suits you."

At last, one day, Old Man decided that he

would make a woman and a child, and he modelled some clay in human shape, and after he had made these shapes and put them on the ground, he said to the clay, "You shall be people." He spread his robe over the clay figures and went away. The next morning he went back to the place and lifted up the robe, and saw that the clay shapes had changed a little. When he looked at them the next morning, they had changed still more; and when on the fourth day he went to the place and took off the covering, he said to the images, "Stand up and walk," and they did so. They walked down to the river with him who had made them, and he told them his name.

As they were standing there looking at the water as it flowed by, the woman asked Old Man, saying, "How is it; shall we live always? Will there be no end to us?"

Old Man said, "I have not thought of that. We must decide it. I will take this buffalo chip and throw it in the river. If it floats, people will become alive again four days after they have died; they will die for four days only. But if it sinks, there will be an end to them." He threw the chip into the river, and it floated.

The woman turned and picked up a stone and said, "No, I will throw this stone in the river. If it floats, we shall live always; if it sinks, people must die, so that their friends who are left alive may always remember them." The woman threw the stone in the water, and it sank.

"Well," said Old Man, "you have chosen; there will be an end to them."

Not many nights after that the woman's child died, and she cried a great deal for it. She said to Old Man, "Let us change this. The law that you first made, let that be the law."

He said, "Not so; what is made law must be law. We will undo nothing that we have done. The child is dead, but it cannot be changed. People will have to die."

These first people did not have hands like a person; they had hands like a bear with long claws. They were poor and naked and did not know how to get a living. Old Man showed them the roots and the berries, and showed them how to gather these, and told them how at certain times of the year they should peel the bark off some trees and eat it; that the little animals that live in the ground—rats, squirrels, skunks, and beavers—were good to eat. He also taught them something about the roots that were good for medicine to cure sickness.

In those days there were buffalo, and these black animals were armed, for they had long horns. Once, as the people were moving about, the buffalo saw them and rushed upon them and hooked them and killed them, and then ate them. One day, as the creator was travelling about, he came upon some of his children that he had made lying there dead, torn to pieces and partly eaten by the buffalo. When he saw this, he felt badly. He said, "I have not made these people right. I will change this; from now on the people shall eat the buffalo."

He went to some of the people who were still alive, and said to them, "How is it that you people do nothing to these animals that are killing you?" The people replied, "What can we do? These animals are armed and can kill us, and we have no way to kill them."

The creator said, "That is not hard. I will make you something that will kill these animals."

He went out and cut some straight service-berry shoots, and brought them in, and peeled the bark from them. He took a larger piece of wood and flattened it, and tied a string to it, and made a bow. Now he was the master of all birds and he went out and caught one, and took feathers from its wings and tied them to the shaft of wood. He tied four feathers along the shaft and tried the arrow at a mark and found that it did not fly well. He took off these feathers and put on three, and when he again tried it at the mark he found that it went straight. He picked up some hard stones, and broke sharp pieces from them. When he tried them he found that the black flint stones made the best arrow points. He showed them how to use these things.

Then he spoke to the people, and said, "The next time you go out, take these things with you, and use them as I tell you. Do not run from these animals. When they rush at you, and have come pretty close, shoot the arrows at them as I have taught you, and you will see that they will run from you or will run around you in a circle."

He also broke off pieces of stone, and fixed them in a handle, and told them that when they killed the buffalo they should cut up the flesh with these stone knives.

One day after this, some people went on a little hill to look about, and the buffalo saw them and called out to each other, "Ah, there is some more of our food," and rushed upon them. The people did not run. They began to shoot at the buffalo with the bows and arrows that had been given them, and the buffalo began to fall. They say that when the first buffalo hit with an arrow felt it prick him, he called out to his fellows, "Oh, my friends, a great fly is biting me."

With the flint knives that had been given them they cut up the bodies of the dead buffalo. About this time Old Man came up and said to them, "It is not healthful to eat raw flesh. I will show you something better than that." He gathered soft, dry rotten wood and made punk of it, and took a piece of wood and drilled a hole in it with an arrow point, and gave them a pointed piece of hard wood, and showed them how to make a fire with fire sticks, and to cook the flesh of animals.

After this the people found a certain sort of stone in the land, and took another harder stone, and worked one upon the other and hollowed out the softer one, so as to make of it a kettle.

It is told also that the creator made people and animals at another place, and in another way. At the Porcupine Mountains he made other earthen images of people, and blew breath on the images, and they became people. They were men and women. After a time they asked him, "What are we to eat?" Then he took more earth and made many images in the form of buffalo, and when he had blown on them they stood up, and he made signs to them and they started to run. He said to the people, "There is your food."

"Well, now," they replied; "we have those animals, how are we to kill them?"

"I will show you," he said.

153

He took them to the edge of a cliff and showed them how to heap up piles of stone, running back from the cliff like this : : : . . . , with the point of the V toward the cliff. He said to the people, "Now, do you hide behind these piles of stones, and when I lead the buffalo this way, as they get opposite to you, stand up."

Then he went on toward a herd of buffalo and began to call them, and the buffalo started toward him and followed him, until they were inside the arms of the V. Then he ran to one side and hid, and as the people rose up the buffalo ran on in a straight line and jumped over the cliff and some of them were killed by the fall.

"There," he said, "go and take the flesh of those animals." Then the people tried to do so. They tried to tear the limbs apart, but they could not. They tried to bite pieces out of the bodies, but they could not do that. Old Man went to the edge of the cliff and broke some pieces of stone with sharp edges, and showed them how to cut the flesh with these. Of the buffalo that went over the cliff, some were not dead, but were hurt, so they could not run away. The people cut strips of green hide and tied stones in the middle, and with these hammers broke in the skulls of the buffalo and killed them.

When they had taken the skins from these animals, they set up poles and put the hides over them, and so made a shelter to sleep under.

In later times the creator marked off a piece of land for the five tribes, Blackfeet, Bloods, Piegans, Gros Ventres, and Sarsis, and said to these tribes, "When people come to cross this line at the border of your land, take your bows and arrows, your lances and your war clubs and give them battle, and keep them out. If they gain a footing here, trouble for you will follow."

OLD MAN STORIES

UNDER the name Na'pi, Old Man, have been confused two wholly different persons talked of by the Blackfeet. The Sun, the creator of the universe, giver of light, heat, and life, and reverenced by every one, is often called Old Man, but there is another personality who bears the same name, but who is very different in his character. This last Na'pi is a mixture of wisdom and foolishness; he is malicious, selfish, childish, and weak. He delights in tormenting people. Yet the mean things he does are so foolish that he is constantly getting himself into scrapes, and is often obliged to ask the animals to help him out of his troubles. His bad deeds almost always bring their own punishment.

Interpreters commonly translate this word Na'pi as Old Man, but it is also the term for white man; and the Cheyenne and Arapahoe tribes tell just such stories about a similar person whom they also call "white man." Tribes of Dakota stock tell of a similar person whom they call "the spider."

The stories about this Old Man are told by the Blackfeet for entertainment rather than with any serious purpose, and when that part of the story is reached where Old Man is in some difficulty which he cannot get out of, the man who is telling the story, and those who are listening to it, laugh delightedly.

Some stories of this kind are these:

THE WONDERFUL BIRD

ONE day, as Old Man was walking about among the trees, he saw something that seemed very queer.

A little bird was sitting on the branch of a tree. Every little while it would make a strange noise, and every time it made this noise its eyes flew out of its head and fastened on a branch of the tree. Then after a little while the bird would make another sort of noise and its eyes would go back to their places in its head.

157

Old Man called out to the bird, "Little brother, teach me how to do that."

"If I show you how," the bird answered, "you must not send your eyes out of your head more than four times in a day. If you do, you will be sorry."

"It shall be as you say, little brother. It is for you to give, and I will listen to what you say."

When the bird had taught Old Man how to do this, he was glad. He began to do it, and did it four times right away. Then he said, "Why did that bird tell me to do this only four times? He has no sense. I will do it again." So once more he made his eyes go out, but now when he called to them they would not come back.

He shouted out to the bird, "Little brother, come here, and help me to get back my eyes." The little bird did not answer him; it had flown away. Now Old Man felt all over the branches of the tree with his hands, but he could not find his eyes. So he went away and wandered over the prairie for a long time, crying and calling to the animals to help him.

As he was blind, he could find nothing to eat, and he began to be very hungry.

A wolf teased him a great deal and had much fun. It had found a dead buffalo, and taking a piece of the meat, it would hold the meat close to Old Man's face. Then Old Man would say, "I smell something dead, I wish I could find it; I am almost starved." He felt all around for it.

Once when the wolf was doing this, Old Man caught him, and plucking out one of the wolf's eyes, he put it in his own head. Then he could see, and was able to find his own eyes, but never again could he do the trick the little bird had taught him.

THE RABBITS' MEDICINE

ONCE, when Old Man was travelling about, he heard some singing that sounded very queer. He had never before heard anything like it, and looked all about to see where it came from. After a time he saw that the cottontail rabbits were singing and making medicine. They had built a fire, and raked out some hot ashes, and they would lie down in these ashes and sing, while one of the others covered them up. They could stay there only for a short time, though, for the ashes were hot.

"Little brothers," said Old Man, "here is something wonderful—that you can lie in those hot ashes and coals without burning. I ask you to teach me how to do this."

"We will show you how to do it, Old Man," said the rabbits. "You must sing our song, and stay in the ashes only a short time." They taught Old Man their song, and he began to sing and lay down, and they covered him with coals and ashes, and the hot ashes did not burn him.

"That is good," he said. "You have strong medicine. Now, so that I may know it all, do you lie down and let me cover you up."

All the rabbits lay down in the ashes, and Old Man covered them up, and then he pulled the whole fire over them. One old rabbit got out, and Old Man was just about to put her back when she said, "Pity me; my children need me."

"It is good," replied Old Man. "You may go, so that there will be more rabbits; but these

I will roast, and have a feast." He put more wood on the fire, and when the rabbits were cooked he got some red willow brush and put the rabbits on it to cool. The grease from their bodies soaked into the branches, so that even to-day if red willow is held over a fire one may see the grease on the bark. Ever since that time, too, the rabbits have a burnt place on the back, where the one that got away was singed.

Old Man sat down by the fire, waiting for the rabbits to get cool, when a coyote came along, limping. He went on three legs. "Pity me, Old Man," he said. "You have plenty of cooked rabbits, give me one of them."

"Go away," said Old Man, very cross; "if you are too lazy to catch food, I will not give you any."

"But my leg is broken," said the coyote; "I cannot run. I cannot catch anything, and I am starving. Give me half a rabbit."

"I don't care what happens to you," said Old Man; "I worked hard to catch and cook these rabbits, and I shall not give any of them away. I'll tell you what I will do, though; I will run a race with you out to that far butte on the prairie, and if you beat me you can have a rabbit."

"Good," said the coyote, and they started.

Old Man ran very fast, and the coyote limped along behind him, but pretty close, until they got near the butte. Then the coyote turned around and ran back very fast, for he was not lame at all. It took Old Man a long time to get back, and just before he reached the fire, the coyote finished eating the last rabbit and ran away.

THE LOST ELK MEAT

OLD MAN had been a long time without food and was very hungry. He was trying to think how he could get something to eat, when he saw a band of elk come up on a ridge. He went over to them and spoke to them and said, "Brothers, I am lonely because I have no one to follow me."

"Go ahead, Old Man," said the elk; "we will follow you." Old Man led them about for a long time, and when it was dark he came near a high, steep cut bank. He ran around to one side, where the hill sloped, and then went back right under the steep cliff and called out, "Come on, that is a nice jump. You will laugh." So all the elk jumped off and were killed, except one cow.

"They have all jumped but you," said Old Man. "Come on, you will like it."

"Take pity on me," said the cow. "I am very heavy, and I am afraid to jump."

"Go away, then," said Old Man; "go and live. Then some day there will be plenty of elk again."

Old Man built a fire and cooked some of the meat, and then he skinned all the elk, and cut up the meat and hung it up to dry. The tongues he hung on a pole.

The next day he started off and was gone all day, and at night, as he was coming home, he was very hungry. He was thinking to himself that he would have some roasted ribs and a tongue and other good things; but when he reached the place, the meat was all gone; the wolves had eaten it.

"It was lucky I hung up those tongues," said

Old Man, "or I should not have had anything to eat." But when he took down the tongues they were all hollow. The mice had eaten out the meat, leaving only the skins.

THE ROLLING ROCK

ONCE when Old Man was travelling about and felt tired, he sat down on a rock to rest. After he was rested he started on his way, and because the sun was hot he threw his robe over the rock and said to it, "Here, I give you my robe because you are poor and have let me rest on you. Keep it always."

He had not gone far when it began to rain, and meeting a coyote, he said to him, "Little brother, run back to that rock and ask him to lend me his robe. We will cover ourselves with it and keep dry."

The coyote ran back to the rock, but presently returned without the robe.

"Where is the robe?" asked Old Man.

"Why," said the coyote, "the rock said that you had given him the robe and he was going to keep it."

This made Old Man angry, and he went back to the rock and snatched the robe off it, saying, "I was only going to borrow this robe until the rain was over, but now that you have acted so mean about it, I will keep it. You don't need a robe, anyhow. You have been out in the rain and snow all your life, and it will not hurt you to live so always."

When he had said this he put the robe about his shoulders, and with the coyote he went off into a ravine and they sat down there. The rain was falling and they covered themselves with the robe, and were warm and dry.

Pretty soon they heard a loud, rumbling noise, and Old Man said to the coyote, "Little brother, go up on the hill and see what that noise is."

The coyote went off, but presently he came back, running as hard as he could, saying, "Run, run, the big rock is coming." They both started, and ran away as fast as they could. The coyote tried to creep into a badger-hole, but it was too small for him and he stuck fast, and before he could get out the rock rolled over him and crushed his hips. Old Man was frightened, and as he ran he threw away his robe and everything that he had on, so that he might run faster. The rock was gaining on him all the time.

Not far away on the prairie a band of buffalo bulls were feeding, and Old Man cried out to them, saying, "Oh, my brothers, help me, help me; stop that rock." The bulls ran and tried to stop it, butting against it, but it crushed their heads. Some deer and antelope tried to help Old Man, but they too were killed. Other animals came to help him, but could not stop the rock; it was now close to Old Man, so close that it began to hit his heels. He was just going to give up when he saw circling over his head a flock of night-hawks.

"Oh, my little brothers," he cried, "help me; I am almost dead." The bull bats flew down one after another against the rock, and every time one of them hit it he chipped off a piece, and at last one hit it fair in the middle and broke it into two pieces.

Then Old Man was glad. He went to where there was a nest of night-hawks and pulled their mouths out wide and pinched off their bills, to make them pretty and queer looking. That is the reason they look so to-day.

BEAR AND BULLBERRIES

SCATTERED over the prairie in northern Montana, close to the mountains, are many great rocks—boulders which thousands of years ago, when the great ice-sheet covered northern North America, were carried from the mountains out over the prairie by the ice and left there when it melted.

Around most of these great boulders the buffalo used to walk from time to time, rubbing against the rough surface of the rock to scratch themselves, as a cow rubs itself against a post or as a horse rolls on the ground—for the pleasant feeling that the rubbing of the skin gives it.

As the buffalo walked around these boulders their hoofs loosened the soil, and this loosened soil—the dust—was blown away by the constant winds of summer. So, around most of these boulders, much of the soil is gone, leaving a deep trench, at the bottom of which are stones and gravel, too large to be moved by the wind.

This story explains how these rocks came to be like that:

Once Old Man was crossing a river and the stream was deep, so that he was carried away by the current, and lost his bow and arrows and other weapons. When he got to the shore he began to look about for something to use in making a bow and arrows, for he was hungry and wanted to kill some food.

He took the first wood he could find and made a bow and arrows and a handle for his knife. When he had finished these things he started on his way.

Presently, as he looked over a hill he saw down below him a bear digging roots. Old Man thought he would have some fun with the bear, and he called out aloud, "He has no tail." Then he dodged back out of sight. The bear looked all about, but saw no one, and again began to dig roots. Then Old Man again peeped over the hill and saw the bear at work, and again called out, "He has no tail." This time the bear looked up more quickly, but Old Man dodged down, and the bear did not see him, and pretty soon went on with his digging.

Four times Old Man did this, calling the bear names, but the fourth time the bear was on the watch and saw Old Man, and started after him.

Old Man ran away as hard as he could, but the bear followed fast. Presently, Old Man tried to shoot the bear with his arrows, but they were made of bad wood and would not fly well, and if they hit the bear, they just broke off. All his weapons failed him, and now the bear was close to him. Just in front was a great rock, and when Old Man came to that, he dodged behind it and ran around to the other side, and the bear followed him. They kept running around the rock for a long time and wore a deep trail about it, and because Old Man could turn more quickly, he kept just ahead of the bear. Old Man kept calling to the animals to help him, but no one came.

He was almost out of breath, and the bear was close to him, when Old Man saw lying on the ground a bull's horn. He picked it up and held it on his head and turned around and bellowed loudly, and the bear was frightened and turned around and ran away as hard as he could. Then Old Man leaned up against the rock, and breathed hard for a long time, but at last he got his wind back. He said to the rock, "This is the way you rocks shall always be after this, with a big hole all around you."

By this time he was pretty tired and thirsty, and he thought he would go down to the river and drink. When he got to the edge of the water he got down on his knees to drink, and there before him in the water he saw bull-berries, great bunches of them. He said to himself, "I will dive in and get those bull-berries"; and he took off his moccasins and clothing and dived in, but he could not find the bullberries, and presently he came up. He looked into the water again, and again saw the bullberries. He said to himself, "Those bullberries must be very deep down."

He went along the shore looking for a heavy stone that would take him down into the deep water where the bullberries were, and when he found one he tied the stone to his neck and again dived in. This time he sank to the bottom, for the stone carried him down. He felt about with his hands trying to reach the bullberries, but could feel nothing and began to drown. He tried to get free from the stone, but that was hard to do; yet at last he broke the string and came to the top of the water. He was almost dead, and it took him a long time to get to the shore, and when he got there he crawled up on to the bank and lay down to rest and get his breath. As he lay there on his back, he saw above him the thick growing bullberries whose reflections he had seen in the water. He said to himself, "And I was almost drowned for these." Then he took a stick and with it began to beat the bullberry bushes. He said to the bushes, "After this, the people shall beat you in this way when they want to gather berries."

The Blackfeet women, when gathering bullberries, spread robes under the bushes and beat the branches with sticks, knocking off the berries, which fall on the robes.

THE THEFT FROM THE SUN

ONE time when Old Man was on a journey, he came to the Sun's lodge, and went in and sat down, and the Sun asked him to stay with him for a time. Old Man was glad to do so. One day the meat was all gone, and the Sun said, "Well, Old Man, what do you say if we go out and kill some deer?"

"I like what you say," said Old Man. "Deer meat is good."

The Sun took down a bag that was hanging from a lodge pole and took from it a handsome pair of leggings, embroidered with porcupine quills and pretty feathers.

"These are my hunting leggings," said the Sun; "they have great power. When I want to kill deer, all I have to do is to put them on and walk around a patch of brush, and the leggings set it on fire and drive out the deer, so that I can shoot them."

"Well, well," exclaimed Old Man, "how wonderful that is!" He began to think, " I wish I had such a pair of leggings as that"; and after he

172

had thought about it some more, he made up his mind that he would have those leggings, if he had to steal them.

They went out to hunt, and when they came to a patch of brush, the Sun set it on fire with his hunting leggings. A number of deer ran out, and each shot one.

That night when they were going to bed the Sun pulled off his leggings, and laid them aside. Old Man saw where he had put them, and in the middle of the night, after every one was asleep, he took the leggings and went away. He travelled a long time, until he had gone far and was tired; then making a pillow of the leggings he lay down and slept. After a while he heard some one speaking and woke up and saw that it was day. Some one was talking to him. The Sun was saying, "Old Man, why are my leggings under your head?"

Old Man looked about him and saw that he was in the Sun's lodge. He thought he must have wandered around and got lost and returned there. Again the Sun spoke, and asked, "What are you doing with my leggings?"

"Oh," replied Old Man, "I could not find anything for a pillow, so I put these leggings under my head."

When night came and all had gone to bed, again Old Man stole the leggings and ran off. This time he did not walk at all. He kept running until it was almost morning, and then lay down and slept. When morning came he found himself still in the Sun's lodge.

You see what a fool he was; he did not know that the whole world is the Sun's lodge. He did not know that, no matter how far he ran, he could not get out of the Sun's sight.

This time the Sun said, "Old Man, since you like my leggings so much, I give them to you. Keep them." Then Old Man was glad and he went away.

One day his food was all gone, and he put on the hunting leggings and went out and set fire to a piece of brush. He was just going to kill some deer that were running out, when he saw that the fire was getting close to him. He ran away as fast as he could, but the fire gained on him and began to burn his legs. His leggings were all on fire. He came to a river and jumped in and pulled off the leggings as soon as he could. They were burnt to pieces.

Perhaps the Sun did this because Old Man tried to steal his leggings.

THE SMART WOMAN CHIEF

LONG ago, they tell me, men and women did not know each other. Women were put in one place and men in another. They were not together; they were apart.

He who made us made women first. He did not make them very well. That is why they are not so strong as men. The men he made better; so that they were strong.

The women were the smartest. They knew the most. They were the first to make piskuns, and to know how to tan hides and to make moccasins. At that time men wore moccasins made from the shank of the buffalo's leg, and robes made of wolfskin. This was all their clothing.

One day when Old Man was travelling about, he came to a camp of men, and stayed there with them for a long time. It was after this that he discovered there were such beings as women.

One time, as he was travelling along, he saw two women driving some buffalo over a cliff. When Old Man got near them, the women were very much frightened. They did not know what kind of animal it was that was coming. Too much scared to run away, they lay down to hide. When Old Man came up to them he thought they were dead, and said, "Here are two women who are dead. It is not good for them to lie out here on the prairie. I must take them to a certain place." He looked them all over to see what had killed them, but could find no wound. He picked up one of the women and carried her along with him in his arms. She was wondering how she could get away. She let her arms swing loose as if she were dead, and at every step Old Man took the arm swung and hit him in the nose, and pretty soon his nose began to bleed and to hurt, and at length he put the woman down on the ground and went back to get the other woman; but while he was gone she had run away, and when he came back to get the first one she was gone too; so he lost them both. This made him angry, and he said to himself, "If these two women will lie there again, I will get both of them."

In this way women found out that there were men.

One day Old Man stood on a hill and looked over toward the piskun at Woman's Falls, where the women had driven a band of buffalo over the cliff, and afterward were cutting up the meat. The chief of the women called him down to the camp, and sent word by him to the men, asking if they wanted to get wives. Old Man brought back word that they did, and the chief woman sent a message, calling all the men to a feast in her lodge to be married. The woman asked Old Man, "How many chiefs are there in that tribe?" He answered, "There are four chiefs. But the real chief of all that tribe you will know when you see him by this—he is finely dressed and wears a robe trimmed, and painted red, and carries a lance with a bone head on each end." Old Man wanted to marry the chief of the women, and intended to dress in this way, and that is why he told her that.

Old Man had no moccasins; his were all worn out. The women gave him some for himself, and also some to take back to give to the men, and he went back to the men's camp. When he reached it, word went out that he had returned, and all the men said to each other, "He has got back; Old Man has come again." He gave the men the message that the woman had sent, and soon the men started for the woman's camp to get married. When they came near it, they went up on a bluff and stood there, looking down on the camp. Old Man had dressed himself finely, and had put on a trimmed robe painted red, and in his hand held a lance with a bone head on each end.

When the women saw that the men had come they got ready to go and select their husbands. The chief of the women said, "I am the chief. I will go first and take the man I like. The rest wait here."

The woman chief started up the hill to choose the chief of the men for her husband. She had been making dried meat, and her hands, arms, and clothing were covered with blood and grease. She was dirty, and Old Man did not know her. The woman went up to Old Man to choose him, but he turned his back on her and would not go with her.

She went back to her camp and told the women that she had been refused because her clothes were dirty. She said, "Now, I am going to put on my nice clothes and choose a man. All of you can go up and take men, but let no one take that man with the red robe and the double-headed lance."

After she was nicely dressed the chief woman again went up on the hill. Now, Old Man knew who she was, and he kept getting in front of her and trying hard to have her take him, but she would not notice him and took another man, the one standing next to Old Man. Then the other women began to come, and they kept coming up and choosing men, but no one took Old Man, and at last all the men were taken and he was left standing there alone.

This made him so angry that he wanted to do

something, and he went down to the woman's piskun and began to break down its walls, so the chief of the women turned him into a pine-tree.

BOBCAT AND BIRCH TREE

ONCE Old Man was travelling over the prairie, when he saw far off a fire burning, and as he drew near it he saw many prairie-dogs sitting in a circle around the fire. There were so many of them that there was no place for any one to sit down. Old Man stood there behind the circle, and presently he began to cry, and then he said to the prairie-dogs, "Let me, too, sit by that fire." The prairie-dogs said, "All right, Old Man, don't cry; come and sit by the fire." They moved aside so as to make a place for him, and Old Man sat down and looked on at what they were doing.

He saw that they were playing a game, and this was the way they did it: they put one prairie-dog in the fire and covered him up with hot ashes, and then, after he had been there a little while, he would say, "*sk, sk,*" and they pushed the ashes off him and pulled him out.

Old Man said, "Little brothers, teach me how to do that." The prairie-dogs told him what to do, and put him in the fire and covered him up with the ashes, and after a little time he said, "*sk, sk*," like a prairie-dog, and they pulled him out again. Then he did it to the prairie-dogs.

At first he put them in one at a time, but there were many of them, and soon he got tired and said, "I will put you all in at once." They said, "Very well, Old Man," and all got in the ashes, but just as Old Man was about to cover them up one of them, a female, said, "Do not cover me up, for I fear the heat will hurt me." Old Man said, "Very well; if you do not wish to be covered up, you may sit over by the fire and watch the rest." Then he covered over all the others.

At length the prairie-dogs said, "*sk, sk*," but Old Man did not sweep off the ashes and pull them out of the fire. He let them stay there and die. The she one that was looking on ran to a hole, and as she went down in it, said, "*sk, sk*." Old Man chased her, but he got to the hole too late to catch her.

"Oh, well, you can go," he said; "there will be more prairie-dogs by and by."

When the prairie-dogs were roasted, Old Man cut some red willow twigs to place them on, and then sat down and began to eat. He ate until he was full, and then felt sleepy.

He said to his nose, "I am going to sleep now; watch out, and in case any bad thing comes about, wake me up." Then Old Man slept.

Pretty soon his nose snored, and Old Man woke up and said, "What is it?" The nose said, "A raven is flying by, over there." Old Man said, "That is nothing," and went to sleep again.

Soon his nose snored again, and Old Man said, "What is it now?" The nose said, "There is a coyote over there, coming this way." Old Man said, "A coyote is nothing," and again went to sleep.

Presently his nose snored again, but Old Man did not wake up. Again it snored, and called out, "Wake up, a bobcat is coming." Old Man paid no attention; he slept on.

The bobcat crept up to the fire and ate all

the roasted prairie-dogs, and then went off and lay down on the flat rock and went to sleep. All this time the nose kept trying to awaken Old Man, and at last he awoke, and the nose said, "A bobcat is over there on that flat rock. He has eaten all your food." Then Old Man was so angry that he called out loud.

The tracks of the bobcat were all greasy from the food it had been eating, and Old Man followed these tracks. He went softly over to where the bobcat was sleeping, and seized it before it could wake up to bite or scratch him. The bobcat cried out, "Wait, let me speak a word or two," but Old Man would not listen.

"I will teach you to steal my food," he said. He pulled off the lynx's tail, pounded his head against the rock so as to make his face flat, pulled him out long so as to make him small-bellied, and then threw him into the brush. As he went sneaking away, Old Man said, "There, that is the way you bobcats shall always be." It is for this reason that the lynxes to-day look like that.

Old Man went to the fire, and looked at the

red willow sticks where the roasted prairie-dogs
had been, and when he saw them, and thought
how his food was all gone, it made him angry
at his nose. He said, "You fool, why did you
not wake me?" He took the willow sticks and
thrust them in the coals, and when they had
caught fire he burnt his nose. This hurt, and
he ran up on a hill and held his nose to the wind,
and called to the wind to blow hard and cool
him. A hard wind came, so hard that it blew
him off the hill and away down to Birch Creek.
As he was flying along he caught at the weeds
and brush to stop himself, but nothing was
strong enough to hold him. At last he grasped
a birch tree. He held fast, and it did not give
way. Although the wind whipped him about,
this way and that, and tumbled him up and
down, the tree held him. He kept calling to the
wind to blow more softly, and at last it listened
to him and went down.

Then he said, "This is a beautiful tree. It
has saved me from being blown away and
knocked all to pieces. I will make it pretty, and
it shall always be like that." So he gashed the

bark across with his stone knife, as you see the marks to-day.

THE RED-EYED DUCK

ONCE, long ago, Old Man was travelling north along a river. He carried a great pack on his back. After a time he came to a place where the river spread out and the water was quiet, and here many ducks were swimming about. Old Man did not look at the ducks, and kept travelling along; but presently some of the ducks saw him and looked at him and said to each other, "Who is that going along there with a pack on his back?" One duck said to the others, "That must be Old Man."

The duck that knew him called out, saying, "Hi, Old Man, where are you going?"

"I am going on farther," replied Old Man, "I have been sent for."

"What have you got in your pack?" said the duck.

"Those are my songs," answered Old Man. "Some people have asked me to come and sing for them."

"Stop for a while and sing for us," said the duck, "and we can have a dance."

"No," said Old Man, "I am in a hurry; I cannot stop now."

The duck kept persuading him to stop, and when it had asked him the fourth time, Old Man stopped and said to the ducks, "Well, I will stop for a little while and sing for you, and you can dance."

So the ducks all came out on the bank and stood in a circle, and Old Man began to sing. He sang one song, and then said, "Now, this next song is a medicine song, and while you dance you must keep your eyes shut. No one must look. If any one opens his eyes and looks, his eyes will turn red."

The ducks closed their eyes and Old Man began to sing, and they danced around; but Old Man took a stick, and every time one of them passed him, he knocked it on the head and threw it into the circle.

Presently one of the littlest ducks while dancing could not feel any one on either side of him, and he opened his eyes and looked, and saw what Old Man was doing. He cried out to the rest, "Run, run, Old Man is killing us"; and all the other ducks flew away, but ever since that time that little duck's eyes have been red. It is the horned grebe.

Old Man took the ducks and went off a little way and built a fire and hung some of the ducks up in front of it to roast, and after the fire was burning well, he swept away the ashes and buried some of the ducks in the ground and again swept back the fire over them. Then he lay down to wait for the birds to cook, and while they were cooking he fell asleep.

While he slept a coyote came sneaking along and saw Old Man sleeping there, and the ducks roasting by the fire. Very quietly he crept up to the fire and took the ducks one by one and ate them. Not one was left. Pretty soon he found those that were roasting under the fire, and dug them out, and opening them, ate the meat from the inside of the skin and filled each one with ashes and buried them all again. Then he went away.

Pretty soon Old Man woke up and saw that

his ducks were gone, and when he saw the tracks about the fire, he knew that the coyote had taken them.

"It was lucky," said Old Man, "that I put some of those to roast under the fire." He dug them up from under the ashes, but when he took a big bite from one, his mouth and face were full of ashes.

THE ANCIENT BLACKFEET

LONG, long ago, before our fathers or grandfathers were born, before the white people knew anything about the western half of
North America, the Indians who told these
stories lived on the Western plains. To the west
of their home rose high mountains, black with
pine-trees on their lower slopes and capped with
snow, but their tents were pitched on the roll-
ing prairie. For a little while in spring this
prairie was green and dotted with flowers, but
for most of the year it stretched away brown
and bare, north, east, and south, farther than one
could see.

On these plains were many kinds of wild animals. Sometimes the prairie was crowded with
herds of black buffalo running in fear; or, again,
the herds, unfrightened, fed scattered out; so
that the hills far and near were dotted with their
dark forms. Among the buffalo were yellow

189

and white antelope—many of them—graceful and swift of foot. Feeding on the high prairie or going down into the wooded river valleys to drink were herds of elk, while the willow thickets, the brushy ravines, and the lower timbered foot-hills sheltered deer. The naked Bad Lands, the rocky slopes of the mountains, and the tall buttes that often rise above the level prairie were the refuge of the mountain sheep, which in those days, like all the other grass eaters of the region, grazed on the prairie and sought the more broken, higher country only when alarmed or when they wished to rest.

These were the animals which the Blackfeet killed for food before the white men came, and of these the buffalo was the chief. Buffalo, more than any other animals, could be captured in numbers, and the Blackfeet, like the other Indians of the plains, had devised a method for taking them, so that when the buffalo were near the Blackfeet never suffered from hunger. Yet sometimes it happened that the buffalo went away, and that the lonely far travelling scouts sent out by the tribe could not find them. Then

the people had to turn to the smaller animals—
the elk, deer, antelope, and wild sheep.

In those old days, before they had horses, they
did not make long marches when they moved.
Their only domestic animal was the dog, which
was used chiefly as a beast of burden, either
carrying loads on its back or hauling a travois,
formed by two long sticks crossing above the
shoulders and dragging on the ground behind.
Behind the dog these two sticks were united by
a little platform, on which was lashed some small
burden—sometimes a little baby.

In those days, when the people moved from
one place to another, all who were large enough
to walk and strong enough to carry a burden on
the shoulders, were laden. Usually men, women,
and children alike bore loads suited to their
strength. Yet sometimes the men carried no
loads at all, for if journeying through a country
where they feared that some enemy might attack them, the men must be ready to fight and
to defend their wives and children. A man
cannot fight well if he is carrying a burden;
he cannot use his arms readily, nor run about

lightly—forward to attack, backward in retreat. If he is not free to fight well, his family will be in danger. White men who have seen Indians journeying in this way, and who have not understood why some women carried heavy loads and the men carried nothing, have said that Indian men were idle and lazy, and forced their women to do all the work. Those who wrote those things were mistaken in what they said. They did not understand what they saw. The truth is that these men were prepared for danger of attacks by enemies, and were ready to do their best to save their families from harm.

Carrying on their backs all their property, except the little which the dogs might pack, it is evident that the Indians in those days could not make long journeys.

In those days they had no buckets of wood or tin in which to carry water. Instead, they used a vessel like a bag or sack, made from the soft membrane of one of the stomachs of the buffalo. This, after it had been cleansed and all the openings from it save one had been tied up, the women filled at the stream with a spoon made of buffalo horn or with a larger ladle of the horn of the wild sheep. Because this water-skin was soft and flexible, it could not stand on the ground, and they hung it up, sometimes on the limb of a tree, more often on one of the poles of the lodge, or sometimes on a tripod—three sticks coming together at the top and standing spread out at the ground.

Most of the meat cooked for the family was roasted, yet much of it was boiled, sometimes in a bowl of stone, sometimes in a kettle made of a fresh hide or of the paunch of the buffalo. Sometimes these skin or paunch kettles were supported at the sides by stakes stuck in the ground, and sometimes a hole dug in the ground was lined with the hide, which was so arranged as to be water-tight. They were not, as may be imagined, put over a fire, but when filled with cold water this water was heated in quite another way. Near by a fire was built, in which were thrown large stones, and on top of the stones more wood was piled; so that after a time, when the wood had burnt down, the stones were very hot—sometimes red hot. With two rather short-handled forked sticks, the women took from the fire one of the hot stones, and put it in the water in the hide kettle, and as it cooled, took it out and put in another hot stone. Thus the water was soon heated, and boiled and cooked whatever was in the kettle. To be sure, there were some ashes and a little dirt in the soup, but that was not regarded as important.

This was long before the Indians knew of matches, or even of flint and steel. In those days to make a fire was not easy and it took a long time. By his knees or feet a man held in position on the ground a piece of soft, dry wood in which two or three little hollows had been dug out, and taking another slender stick of hard wood, and pressing the point in one of the little hollows in the stick of soft wood, he twirled the stick rapidly between the palms of his hands, so fast and so long that presently the dust ground from the softer stick, falling to one side in a little pile, began to smoke, and at last a faint spark was seen at the top of the pile, which began to glow, and, spreading, became constantly larger. He, or his companion, for often two men twirled the stick, one relieving the other, caught this spark in a bit of tinder—perhaps some dry punk or a little fine grass—and by blowing coaxed it into flame, and there was the fire.

This fire making was hard work, and the people tried to escape this work by keeping a spark of fire always alive. To do this, men sometimes carried, by a thong slung over the shoulder, the hollow tip of a buffalo horn, the opening of which was closed by a wooden plug. When going on a journey, the man lighted a piece of punk, and, placing it in this horn, plugged up the open end, so that no air could get into the horn. There the punk smouldered for a long time, and neither went out nor was wholly consumed. Once in a while during the day the man looked at this punk, and, if he saw that it was almost consumed, he lighted another piece and put it in the horn and replaced the plug. So at night when he reached camp the fire was still in his horn, and he could readily kindle a blaze, and from this blaze other fires were kindled. Often, if the camp was large, the first young men who reached it gathered wood and perhaps kindled four fires, and after the women had reached the camp, unpacked their dogs, and put up their lodges, each woman would go to one of these fires to get a brand or some coals with which to start her own lodge fire.

In warm weather men and boys wore little clothing. They went almost naked; yet in cold weather each man or woman was most of the time wrapped in a warm robe of tanned buffalo skin. Even the little children wore robes, the smallest ones those taken from the little buffalo calves. All their clothing, like their beds and their homes, was made of the skins of animals, Shirts, women's dresses, leggings, and moccasins were made from the tanned skins of buffalo, deer, antelope, and mountain sheep. Often the moccasins were made from the smoked skin cut from the top of an old lodge, for this skin had been smoked so much that it never dried hard and stiff, after it had been wet. The moccasins had a stiff sole of buffalo rawhide; and in the bottom of this sole were cut one or two holes, in order that the water might run out if a man had to wade through a stream.

The homes of these Indians were lodges—tents made of tanned buffalo skin supported on a cone of long, straight, slender poles. At the top where the poles crossed was an opening for the smoke from the fire built in the centre of the circular lodge floor, while about the fire, and close under the lodge covering, were the beds where the people slept or ate during the day.

These homes were warm and comfortable. The border of the lodge covering did not come down quite to the ground, but inside the lodge poles, and tied to them, was a long wide strip of tanned buffalo skin four or five feet high, and long enough to reach around the inside of the lodge, almost from one side of the door to the other. This strip of tanned skin—made up of several pieces—was so wide that one edge rested on the floor, and reached inward under the beds and seats. Through the open space between the lodge covering and the lodge lining, fresh air kept passing into the lodge close to the ground and up over the lining and down toward the centre of the lodge, and so furnished draught for the fire. The lodge lining kept this cold air from blowing directly on the occupants of the lodge who sat around the fire. Often the lodge lining was finely painted with pictures of animals, people, and figures of mysterious beings of which one might not speak.

The seats and beds in this home were covered with soft tanned buffalo robes, and at the head and foot of each bed was an inclined back-rest of straight willow twigs, strung together on long lines of sinew and supported in an inclined position by a tripod. Buffalo robes often hung over these back-rests. In the spaces between the back-rests, which though they came together at the top were separated at the ground, were kept many of the possessions of the family; the pipe, sacks of tobacco, of paint, "possible sacks" —parfleches for clothing or food, and many smaller articles.

The outside of the lodge was often painted with mysterious figures which the lodge owner believed to have power to bring good luck to him and to his family. Sometimes these figures represented animals—buffalo, deer, and elk—or rocks, mountains, trees, or the puff-balls that grow on the prairie. Sometimes a procession of ravens, marching one after the other, was painted around the circumference of the lodge. The painting might show the tracks of animals, or a number of water animals, apparently chasing each other around the lodge. On either side of the smoke hole at the top were two flaps, or wings, each one supported by a single pole. These were to regulate the draught of the fire in case of a change of wind, and the poles were moved from side to side, changing as the direction of the wind changed. On such wings were often painted groups of white disks which represented some group of stars. At the back of the lodge, high up, just below the place where the lodge poles cross, was often a large round disk representing the sun, and above that a cross, which was the sign of the butterfly, the power that they believe brings sleep. From the ends of the wings, or tied to the tips of the poles which supported them, hung buffalo tails, and sometimes running down from one of these poles

199

to the ground near the door was a string of the sheaths of buffalo hooflets, which rattled as it swung to and fro in the breeze.

Their arms were the bow and arrow, a short spear or lance, with a head of sharpened stone or bone, stone hammers with wooden handles, and knives made of bone or stone, and if of stone, lashed by rawhide or sinew to a split wooden handle.

The hammers were of two sorts: one quite heavy, almost like a sledge-hammer or maul, and with a short handle; the other much lighter, and with a longer, more limber handle. This last was used by men in war as a mace or war club, while the heavier hammer was used by women as an axe to break up fallen trees for firewood; as a hammer to drive tent-pins into the ground, to kill disabled animals, or to break up heavy bones for the marrow they contained. These mauls and hammers were usually made by choosing an oval stone and pecking a groove about its shortest diameter. The handles were made by green sticks fitted as closely as possible into the groove, brought together and lashed in position by sinew, the whole being then covered with wet rawhide tightly fitted and sewed. As the rawhide dried, it shrunk and strongly bound together the parts of the weapon.

The Blackfeet bow was about four feet long. Its string was of twisted sinew and it was backed with sinew. This gave the bow great power, so that the arrow went with much force. The arrows were straight shoots of the service berry or cherry, and the manufacture of arrows was the chief employment of many of the men of middle life. Each arrow by the same maker was precisely like every other arrow he made. Each arrowmaker tried hard to make good arrows. It was a fine thing to be known as a maker of good arrows.

The shoots for the arrow shafts were brought into the lodge, peeled, smoothed roughly, tied up in bundles, and hung up to dry. After they were dried, the bundles were taken down and each shaft was smoothed and reduced to a proper thickness by the use of a grooved piece of sandstone, which acted on the arrow like sandpaper. After they were of the right thickness, they were straightened by bending with the hands, and sometimes with the teeth, and were then passed through a circular hole drilled in a rib, or in a mountain sheep's horn, which acted in part as a gauge of the size and also as a smoother, for if in passing through the hole the arrow fitted tightly, the shaft received a good polish. The three grooves which always were found in the Blackfeet arrows were made by pushing the shaft through a round hole drilled in a rib, which, however, had one or more projections left on the inside. These projections pressed into the soft wood and made the grooves, which were in every arrow. The feathers were three in number. They were put on with a glue, made by boiling scraps of dried rawhide, and were held in place by wrappings of sinew. The heads of the arrows were made of stone or bone or horn. The flint points were often highly worked and very beautiful, being broken from larger flints by sharp blows of a stone hammer, and after they had been shaped the edges were worked sharp by flaking with an implement of bone or horn. The points made of horn or bone were ground sharp by rubbing on a stone. A notch was cut in the end of the arrow shaft and the shank of the arrow point set in that. The arrow heads were firmly fixed to the shaft by glue and by sinew wrapping.

Although the Blackfeet lived almost altogether on the flesh of birds or animals, yet they had some vegetable food. This was chiefly berries—of which in summer the women collected great quantities and dried them for winter use—and roots, the gathering of which at the proper season of the year occupied much of the time of women and young girls. These roots were unearthed by a long, sharp-pointed stick, called a root digger. Some of the roots were eaten as soon as collected, while others were dried and stored for use in winter.

After they reached the plains, the main food of the Blackfeet was the buffalo, which they killed in large numbers when everything went right. Many of the streams in the Blackfeet country run through wide, deep valleys bordered on either side by cliffs, or broken precipices, falling sharply from the high prairie above. Long ago the Blackfeet must have learned that it was possible to make the buffalo jump over these cliffs, and that in the fall on the rocks below numbers would be killed or crippled. No doubt after this had been practised for a time, there came to some one the idea of building at the foot of such a cliff where the buffalo were run over, a fence which would form a corral or pound, and which would hold all the buffalo that were jumped over the cliff. This corral they called piskun.

It is often said that the buffalo were driven over these precipices, but this is true only in part. Like most wild animals, buffalo are inquisitive. It was not difficult to excite their curiosity, and when they saw something they did not recognize, they were anxious to find out what it was.

When run into the piskun, the buffalo were really drawn by curiosity almost to the jumping point, and between two long diverging lines of people, who kept hidden until after the buffalo had passed them, and then rose and showed themselves and tried to frighten the animals. Now, to be sure, for the short distance that remained between the place where they were alarmed and the place where they jumped, the buffalo were driven. Any attempt on the open prairie to drive buffalo in one direction or another would be certain to fail. The animals would go where they wished to. They would not be driven, though often they might be led.

To the people the capture of food was the most important thing in life, and they put forth every effort to accomplish it. For this reason it came about that the effort to capture buffalo was preceded usually by religious ceremonies, in which many prayers were offered to the powers of the earth, the sky, and the waters, many sacrifices made, and sacred objects, like the buffalo stone, were displayed.

When the day for the hunt came, the man who was to bring the buffalo left the camp early in the morning, climbed the rocky bluffs to the high prairie, and journeyed toward some near-by herd of buffalo, that had been located the day before by himself or by other young men. He approached the buffalo as nearly as he could without frightening them, and then, attracting the attention of some of the animals by uttering certain calls, tossed into the air his buffalo robe or some smaller object. As soon as the buffalo began to look at him, he retreated slowly in the direction of the piskun, but continued to call and to attract their attention by showing himself and then disappearing. Soon, some of the buffalo began to walk toward him, and others began to look and to follow those that had first started, so that before long the whole herd of fifty or a hundred animals might be walking or sometimes trotting after him. The more rapidly the buffalo came on, the faster the man ran— and sometimes it was a hard matter for him to keep ahead of the herd—until he had got far within the wings and near to the cliff. If there seemed danger that he would be overtaken, he watched his chance and either at some low place quickly dodged out of the line in which the buffalo were running, or hid behind one of the piles of stones of which the wings were formed, or, if he had time, slipped over the rocky wall at the valley's edge, so as to get out of the way of the approaching herd.

As soon as the buffalo had come well within the diverging lines of people who were hidden behind the piles of stones called wings, those whom the buffalo passed rose up from their places of concealment, and by yells and shouts and the waving of their robes frightened the buffalo, so that they quite forgot their curiosity in the terror that now replaced it. When the leaders reached the brink of the cliff, they could not stop. They were pushed over by those behind, and most of the buffalo jumped over the cliff. Many were crippled or injured by the fall, and all were kept within the fence of the piskun below. About this fence the people were collected. The buffalo raced round and round within the pen, the young and weak being injured or killed in the crowding, while above the fence men were shooting them with arrows until presently all in the pen were dead, or so hurt that the women could go into the pen and kill them. The people entered and took the flesh and hides.

Deer, elk, and antelope were shot with arrows, and antelope were often captured in pitfalls roofed with slender poles and covered with grass and earth. Such pitfalls were dug in a region where antelope were plenty, and a long ▷ shaped pair of wings, made of poles or bushes or even rock piles, led to the pit. The antelope is very inquisitive and was easily led within the chute and there frightened, as were the buffalo, by people who had been concealed and who rose up and showed themselves after the antelope had passed. This was done more in order to secure antelope skins for clothing than their flesh for food.

Fish and reptiles were not eaten by the Blackfeet, nor were dogs, although dogs, wolves, and coyotes are eaten by many tribes of plains Indians. Most small animals, and practically all birds, were eaten in case of need. In summer, when the wildfowl which bred on so many of the lakes in the Blackfeet country lost their flight-feathers, during the moult, and again in the late summer, when the young ducks and geese were almost fullgrown but could not yet fly, the Indians often went in large parties to the shallow lakes which here and there dotted the prairie, and, driving the birds to shore, killed them in large numbers.

Earlier in the season, when the fowl had begun to lay their eggs, these were collected in great quantities for food. Sometimes they were roasted in the hot ashes, but a more common way was to dig a deep, narrow hole in the ground in which the eggs were to be cooked. Several little platforms of small sticks or twigs were built in this hole, one above another, and on these platforms they put the eggs. Another much smaller hole was dug to one side of the large hole, slanting down into it. The large hole was partly filled with water, and was then roofed over by small sticks on which was placed grass covered with earth. Stones were heated in a fire built near at hand, and then were rolled down the side hole into the larger hole, heating the water, which at last boiled and steamed, the steam cooking the eggs.

When the Americans first met them on the prairie, the Blackfeet were known as great warriors. But up to the time when they got from the Hudson Bay traders better weapons than they had before known, whether these were metal knives, steel arrow points, or guns, it is probable that they did not do much fighting. There seems to have been no reason why they should have fought, unless they quarrelled about small matters with other tribes. It became quite different when the Indians procured better arms and, above all, when they got horses— a means of swiftly getting about over the country, something that all people wanted to have and which all were so eager to obtain that they would go into danger for them. In the old days of stone arrow heads, when they had to travel on foot and to carry heavy loads on their backs, the whole thought and effort of the tribe must have been devoted to the work of procuring a supply of food.

The tribal and family life of the people was simple and friendly. The man and his wives loved each other and loved their children. Relationship counted for much in an Indian camp, and cousins of remote degree were called brother and sister. Children were not punished; they were trained by persuasion and advice. They were told by older people how they ought to act in order to make their lives happy and successful and to be well thought of by their fellows. Young people had much respect for their elders, listened to what they said, and strove more or less successfully to follow their teachings.

The Blackfeet were very religious. They feared many natural powers and influences whose workings they did not understand, and they were constantly praying to the Sun—regarded as the ruler of the universe—as well as to those other powers which they believe live in the stars, the earth, the mountains, the animals, and the trees. The Blackfoot was constantly afraid that some evil thing might happen to him, and he therefore prayed to all the powers for help—for good fortune in his undertakings, for health, plenty, and long life for himself and all his family.

Among these tribes there are a number of secret societies known as the All Comrades or All Friends—groups of men of different ages, which have been alluded to in the stories. Originally there were about twelve of these societies, but a number have been abandoned of recent years.

The tribe was divided into a number of clans, all the members of which were believed to be related, and in old times no member of a clan was permitted to marry another member of the clan. Relations might not marry.

In olden times, when large numbers of people were together, the lodges of the camp were pitched in a great circle, the opening toward the southeast. In this circle each clan camped in its own particular place with relation to the other clans. Within the circle was often a smaller circle of lodges, each occupied by one or more of the societies of the All Comrades. Sometimes it happened that great numbers of the Blackfeet came together, perhaps even all of the three tribes, Blackfeet, Bloods, and Piegans. When this was the case, each tribe camped by itself with its own circle, no matter how near it might be to one or other of the tribal circles.

We read of some tribes of Indians which believed that after death the spirits of the departed went to a happy hunting ground where game was always plenty and life was full of joy. The Blackfeet knew no such place as this. When they died their spirits were believed to go to a barren, sandy region south of the Saskatchewan, which they called the Sand Hills. Here, as shadows, the ghosts lived a life much like their existence before death, but all was unreal—unsubstantial. Riding on shadow horses they hunted shadow buffalo. They lived in shadow camps and when they moved shadow dogs hauled their travois. There are stories which tell that living people have seen these hunters, their houses, and their implements of the camp, but when the people got close they found that what they thought they had seen was something different. It reminds us a little of the old ballad of Alice Brand, where Urgan tells of the things seen in fairy-land:

> " And gayly shines the Fairy-land—
>   But all is glistening show,
>   Like the idle gleam that December's beam
>   Can dart on ice and snow.
>
> " And fading, like that varied gleam,
>   Is our inconstant shape,

Who now like knight and lady seem,
And now like dwarf and ape."

Books have been written about the Blackfeet Indians which tell much more about how they lived than can be given here.

END